DISK WITH WORKBOOK TO ACCOMPANY WRITTEN EXPRESSION: THE PRINCIPAL'S SURVIVAL GUIDE

India J. Podsen

Routledge
Taylor & Francis Group

New York London

First published 1997 by Eye On Education

Published 2013 by Routledge
711 Third Avenue, New York, NY, 10017, USA
2 Park Square, Milton Park, Abingdon, Oxon OX14 4RN

Routledge is an imprint of the Taylor & Francis Group, an informa business

ISBN: 978-1-883001-42-1 (pbk)

THE SCHOOL PORTFOLIO:
A Comprehensive Framework for School Improvement
By Victoria L. Bernhardt

THE ADMINISTRATOR'S GUIDE TO
SCHOOL-COMMUNITY RELATIONS
By George E. Pawlas

ORGANIZATIONAL OVERSIGHT:
Planning and Scheduling for Effectiveness
By David A. Erlandson, Peggy L. Stark, and Sharon M. Ward

MOTIVATING OTHERS:
Creating the Conditions
By David P. Thompson

INTERPERSONAL SENSITIVITY
By John R. Hoyle and Harrison M. Crenshaw

ORAL AND NONVERBAL EXPRESSION
By Ivan Muse

LEADERSHIP:
A Relevant a Realistic Role for Principals
By Gary Crow, Joseph Matthews, and Lloyd McCleary

JUDGMENT:
Making the Right Calls
By Jim Sweeney and Diana Bourisaw

PROBLEM ANALYSIS:
Responding to School Complexity
By Charles M. Achilles, John S. Reynolds, and Susan H. Achilles

THE SCHOOL LEADERSHIP LIBRARY

The School Leadership Library was designed to show practicing and aspiring principals what they should know and be able to do to be effective leaders of their schools. The books in this series were written to answer the question, "How can we improve our schools by improving the effectiveness of our principals?"

Success in the principalship, like in other professions, requires mastery of a knowledge and skills base. One of the goals of the National Policy Board for Educational Administration (sponsored by NAESP, NASSP, AASA, ASCD, NCPEA, UCEA, and other professional organizations) was to define and organize that knowledge and skill base. The result of our efforts was the development of a set of 21 "domains," building blocks representing the core understanding and capabilities required of successful principals.

The 21 domains of knowledge and skills are organized under four broad areas: Functional, Programmatic, Interpersonal, and Contextual. They are as follows:

FUNCTIONAL DOMAINS
- Leadership
- Information Collection
- Problem Analysis
- Judgment
- Organizational Oversight
- Implementation
- Delegation

PROGRAMMATIC DOMAINS
- Instruction and the Learning Environment
- Curriculum Design
- Student Guidance and Development
- Staff Development
- Measurement and Evaluation
- Resource Allocation

INTERPERSONAL DOMAINS
- Motivating Others
- Interpersonal Sensitivity
- Oral and Nonverbal Expression
- Written Expression

CONTEXTUAL DOMAINS
- Philosophical and Cultural Values
- Legal and Regulatory Applications
- Policy and Political Influences
- Public Relations

These domains are not discrete, separate entities. Rather, they evolved only for the purpose of providing manageable descriptions of essential content and practice so as to better understand the entire complex role of the principalship. Because human behavior comes in "bunches" rather than neat packages, they are also overlapping pieces of a complex puzzle. Consider the domains as converging streams of behavior that spill over one another's banks but that all contribute to the total reservoir of knowledge and skills required of today's principals.

The School Leadership Library was established by General Editors David Erlandson and Al Wilson to provide a broad examination of the content and skills in all of the domains. The authors of each volume in this series offer concrete and realistic illustrations and examples, along with reflective exercises. You will find their work to be of exceptional merit, illustrating with insight the depth and interconnectedness of the domains. This series provides the fullest, most contemporary, and most useful information available for the preparation and professional development of principals.

Scott Thomson, Executive Secretary
National Policy Board for Educational
Administration

PREFACE

This workbook provides principals with the tools they need to put into practice the concepts outlined in *Written Expression: the Principal's Survival Guide*, a volume in Eye On Education's hardcover series, The School Leadership Library. The workbook expands the topics covered in the hardcover book and provides additional examples.

On the diskette you will find many of the sample documents printed in both the hardcover book and this workbook. You may use these files as templates for your own writing tasks.

School administrators identify 10 problem areas in their writing. They are:

1. Conciseness

2. Clarity of meaning

3. Success in communicating the purpose

4. Spelling

5. Sentence clarity and variation

6. Paragraph organization

7. Document organization

8. Sensitivity to the audience's perspective

9. Awareness of the needs of the reader

10. Awareness of tone

TO THE SCHOOL ADMINISTRATOR

This workbook is a resource guide that has been designed as a way for you to develop your game plan in attacking your writing tasks. Its purpose is threefold:

♦ to help you reassess what you need to know about effective writing

♦ to emphasize the types of writing that principals use on the job

♦ to point out strategies that will help you in writing these products faster and with confidence.

We begin in Part One—*Preparation for Training*—with exercises that focus on your current writing attitude and daily writing behaviors on the job. This analysis sets the stage for the information provided on five critical writing dimensions every writer needs to know about and the writing behaviors and strategies we think will help you master your writing tasks.

In Part Two—*Competency Training Modules*—we present the writing types principals encounter on the job. We took the "what you need to know approach" in featuring each type of writing. Every training module presents all or a combination of the following elements:

♦ key information on the writing form

♦ before and after samples to review

♦ document analyses to highlight effective writing strategies

♦ practice exercises to reinforce effective writing behaviors

♦ document templates to get you started faster

In Part Three of the guide—*Initiating the Development Process*— we outline a step-by-step process to help you build on your writing strengths and target growth areas. Personal and professional growth are intertwined; both take planning, effort, and persistence. We encourage you to examine your school's communication effectiveness as well as your own.

TO THE INSTRUCTOR

Our purpose in writing the text, *Written Expression: The Principal's Survival Guide*, and this accompanying disk with workbook was to foster supervisory success in schools through systematic and effective written expression. Both volumes focus on the audiences and types of writing school administrators face on the job.

If you are a staff development coordinator, the competency training modules stand alone and can be used to develop short inservice workshops targeted to a particular audience or writing problem.

For preservice instruction in administrator preparation programs, both the textbook and the workbook provide essential information on effective written communication and successful practice. Whether you are on the quarter system or the semester system, the textbook chapters and workbook competency modules can be assigned to meet the time constraints you face in your academic setting.

The numerous developmental exercises expose the aspiring school administrator to job related situations and problems they will encounter. For veteran administrators, these same exercises provide a way to assess current skill functioning in order to continue their professional growth and to build the overall communication effectiveness of their schools. Individual instructors are encouraged to make their own choices according to their own expertise and experience.

How to Use the Disk

Packaged on the back cover of this workbook are two diskettes: one in Macintosh format, the other for Windows/Windows '95. The files may be opened using any word processing package.

Each of the folders ("directories" for Windows 3.1 users) corresponds to one of the *Competency Training Modules* in Part Two of this workbook. Each file contains one of the documents or templates displayed in this workbook or in the accompanying hardcover book, *Written Expression: The Principals' Survival Guide* (ISBN 1-883001-34-X).

On page 181 of the workbook, you will find "What's on the Disk?" which lists all the folders and files on the disk, cross-referenced to the appropriate pages in the books. After you open one of these files, the document will appear on your computer's screen, allowing you to work interactively with the material in this workbook and build a document file of your own.

You are welcome to copy the files, customize them, save them under other names, and otherwise use them to enhance the quality of your professional writing.

Writing can be easy. Explore your potential!

ABOUT THE AUTHOR

India J. Podsen is Associate Professor of Middle/Secondary Education at North Georgia College and State University in Dahlonega, Georgia. Prior to this position she co-directed and then directed the Principals Center at Georgia State University in Atlanta for ten years. This book grew out of Podsen's 25 years of professional experiences as an English teacher, school administrator, staff developer in leadership training, assessment center director, and consultant to the National Association of Secondary School Principals (NASSP).

TABLE OF CONTENTS

PROLOGUE:
INSIDE THE PRINCIPAL'S OFFICE

Mr. Bentley, the principal of Anywhere School, has had a terrible day. His morning began with a flat tire just after he left home and he was already running late. Frustration mounted when he got to the school parking lot and found his parking place taken by an unknown car.

That was just the beginning. Things continued downhill: two very irate parents waited to see him as he entered the main office, a dozen urgent phone calls from the central office, the school newsletters late from the printer, and four teachers absent with only three substitutes available.

And on top of this, the superintendent called and wanted a status report on his school improvement goals ASAP for an upcoming board meeting.

Bill Bentley held his breath and began his deep breathing exercises, lowering his blood pressure which he knew was climbing into the red zone. Bill has been here before and knows that "this too shall pass." Meanwhile, in handling the events of the day, his in-basket has been pushed to the side.

Later, with his wife and children watching television and his late dinner downed, Bill sits in his study and stares at the pile of stuff that has accumulated in his in-basket. The task seems endless: every letter and memo is different; each request and complaint wanting an immediate and satisfactory response. Bill's mind goes blank. His analytical skills are short-circuited by the task of simply reading the information, let alone responding. But the bottom line is this: Bill finds writing difficult and time consuming. He avoids writing whenever given the choice. When the avoidable becomes unavoidable, he's left dealing with his writing tasks, at home, ALONE.

Bill has fallen into a pattern that is repeated each day by many school administrators who just don't like to write. Without being aware of it, and faced with multiple writing tasks simultaneously, the reluctant writer keeps putting them off, especially the more difficult ones, until the last minute. Then when there is no time left to plan the writing task, the reluctant writer responds. The product, however, often results in a message that is irrelevant and poorly organized.

The purpose of this book is to help administrators like Bill Bentley improve their writing skills, perform writing tasks with more confidence, and generally attack their in-baskets more successfully.

PART ONE

PREPARATION FOR TRAINING

1

FACING YOUR WRITING FEARS

"All glory comes from daring to begin."
—Eugene F. Ware
NASSP Great Quotations

As a school administrator you have developed a large variety of personal and technical tools for dealing with the world around you. You have successfully designed thousands of routines and procedures for handling the day-to-day problems of life, from your private life to your professional life. These are your skills, abilities, and personal characteristics. You wouldn't have made it this far if you didn't have them.

And, in the midst of all this, you have developed your own personal agenda of things that turn you on or turn you off: situations that challenge you, sensations that amuse you, types of relationships that nurture you (or scare you), environments in which you feel comfortable or avoid, activities that contribute to your well-being.

School leaders, in our opinion, who have current information about productive work cultures are far more likely to develop their school's capacity to improve achievement. Similarly, school leaders who have current knowledge about their work skills are far more likely to develop a systematic plan to improve their personal performance.

In this section of the guide you will determine your own areas of strength as they pertain to competence in the field of written expression. We hope the result of your analysis will enable you to set specific learning goals as you engage in the writing exercises interspersed throughout the workbook. As you set these learning goals, consider your perception needs and your skill needs; both are necessary for professional development.

3

CONFRONTING YOUR WRITING APPREHENSION

Despite the emphasis placed on the importance of the role of written communication, many well-educated professionals are ineffective writers. Even effective school administrators find writing a difficult task. Yet, the skill is essential for both personal and professional success.

Conrad (1985) asserts that people who have developed a wide repertoire of written and oral communication skills and who have learned when and how to use those skills tend to advance in their careers more rapidly and contribute more fully to the organization than people who have not done so.

School principals must face daily the demand for some form of writing: letters, memos, bulletins, notices, announcements, guides, speeches, and handbooks. Because of this demand, barriers that reduce writing competence should be examined. One such barrier is writing apprehension.

According to Daly (1985), many people are hesitant about and fearful of writing. This apprehension is often reflected in their writing performance. He emphasizes that the way in which individuals write, and even whether or not they engage in writing at all, depends on more than just skill or writing proficiency. The individual must want to write or, at the very least, find some value in writing. Daly concludes that one's attitude toward writing is just as important to good writing as one's actual writing ability.

Exercise 1.1
WRITING ATTITUDE SURVEY

Let's examine your attitude about writing. Below are a series of statements about writing. There are no right or wrong answers to these statements. Indicate the degree to which each statement applies to you by circling whether you *(1) Strongly Agree, (2) Agree, (3) Are Uncertain, (4) Disagree,* or *(5) Strongly Disagree.* Take your time and try to be as honest as possible.

		SA 1	A 2	U 3	D 4	SD 5	SC Score
*1	I avoid writing whenever possible. *	1	2	3	4	5	
2	I have no fear of my writing being evaluated.	1	2	3	4	5	
3	I look forward to writing down my ideas.	1	2	3	4	5	

*4	I am afraid of writing when I know it might be evaluated.*	1	2	3	4	5	
*5	My mind seems to go blank when I start writing.*	1	2	3	4	5	
*6	Expressing ideas through writing seems to be wasting time.*	1	2	3	4	5	
7	I would enjoy submitting my writing to magazines for evaluation and publication.	1	2	3	4	5	
8	I like to write my ideas down.	1	2	3	4	5	
9	I feel confident in my ability to express clearly my ideas in writing.	1	2	3	4	5	
10	I like to have my friends read what I have written.	1	2	3	4	5	
*11	I'm nervous about writing *	1	2	3	4	5	
12	People seem to enjoy what I write.	1	2	3	4	5	
13	I enjoy writing.	1	2	3	4	5	
*14	I never seem to be able to write down my ideas clearly.*	1	2	3	4	5	
15	Writing is a lot of fun.	1	2	3	4	5	
16	I like seeing my thoughts on paper.	1	2	3	4	5	
17	Discussing my writing with others is an enjoyable experience.	1	2	3	4	5	
18	It is easy for me to write good letters.	1	2	3	4	5	
*19	I don't think I write as well as most people.*	1	2	3	4	5	

*20	I'm no good at writing.*	1	2	3	4	5	
	TOTAL						

Adapted from the Daly-Miller Writing Apprehension Scale in *When a Writer Can't Write*, Edited by Mike Rose, The Guilford Press, New York, 1985, p. 46. Reprinted with permission.

Directions for Scoring: Enter the number you circled in the SC column for each statement. *In scoring the items marked with the asterisk, you need to reverse the score.* For example, if you circled 5 in responding to number #20, then you would mark a 1 in the SC column. Items scored a 3, stay the same. Once you have scored each of the items, total your score and place it in the box at the bottom of the SC column. The lowest score you can get is 20 and the highest score is 100.

Your response to the survey indicates your level of writing apprehension. A score of 20 shows very low writing apprehension; a score of 100 shows very high writing apprehension. Where do you fall on the continuum? Mark your score.

LOW (20-39) _____

MODERATE (40-68) _____

HIGH (69-100) _____

SELF-ASSESSMENT PROFILE

Your attitude about writing sets the stage for many of the tasks facing you as a school administrator. Our experience with hundreds of principals who have participated in NASSP's writing program *From the Desk of...* discloses that while most principals are anxious about their writing and fear evaluation of their documents, the feedback they receive during the workshop improves their attitude by providing specific information on their writing strengths (and there are many) as well as areas for growth.

Exercise 1.2
WRITING BEHAVIOR INVENTORY

Let's continue the self-assessment process by focusing on your writing behaviors. Please respond to each item accurately and honestly using one of the following responses: *Always Do (AD), Generally Do (GD), Sometimes Do (SD),* or *Never Do (ND).*

WRITING BEHAVIORS	AD	GD	SD	ND
1. I set aside a specific time during the day to work on writing tasks.				
2. I gather information I need before I begin writing.				
3. I use prewriting techniques to generate ideas. (Ex. outlining, mindmapping, freewriting)				
4. I identify the specific purpose for each document.				
5. I usually develop a working draft.				
6. I review my draft for style, purpose, and audience.				
7. I develop a second draft.				
8. I proofread to check for common writing errors.				
9. I am sensitive to my audience's problem or concern.				
10. I avoid educational jargon.				
11. My writing presents a professional image.				
12. I have developed routines to organize incoming paperwork and answer routine correspondence.				
13. I use a computer to produce my written materials.				
14. I submit all written reports on time.				
15. I collaborate with staff on documents.				
16. I often seek feedback on my documents.				
TOTAL				

These items correspond to the writing behaviors of effective writers. Analyze your writing patterns. Any areas you have marked *never do* and *sometimes do* may be areas that need to be investigated. For further explorations of these topics, we recommend reading Audrey Joyce's book, *Written Communications and the School Administrator.* The author provides detailed content and specific examples to assist you in expanding your knowledge and skill in performing these behaviors.

Let's continue by analyzing your communication patterns with the various audiences that principals encounter on the job.

Exercise 1.3
PRINCIPAL'S WRITING INVENTORY

Directions: Below are statements about writing. The purpose of the inventory is to help you determine the variety of writing activities and audiences you engage in on the job. There are no right or wrong answers. Check only one response. A NO response shows an activity that you are not doing now. A DELEGATED response indicates a writing task that you do but have assigned to someone else. A YES response shows an activity that you are doing now. For both DELEGATED and YES responses please circle how often you do this writing task: *D-daily, W-weekly, M-monthly, Q-quarterly,* and *Y-yearly.* Take your time and try to be as accurate as possible.

STAFF	NO	YES	DEL	DWM	QY
1. I write a staff newsletter.					
2. I develop teacher handbooks.					
3. I have a substitute teacher guide.					
4. I develop staff surveys.					
5. I write summaries of school board meetings.					
6. I prepare written agendas before staff meetings.					
7. I respond in writing to staff concerns.					
8. I write thank you notes.					
9. I send special occasion cards and notes.					
10. I generate school calendars.					
11. I reinforce verbal requests.					
12. I write letters of recommendation.					
13. I document teacher/staff behaviors in writing.					
14. I write descriptive narratives of teacher performance.					
15. I script classroom observations.					
16. I write letters of staff commendation.					
TOTAL YOUR YES/ NO/ DEL/ RESPONSES					

PARENTS	NO	YES	DEL	DWM	QY
1. I write welcome letters to new parents.					
2. I write a school newsletter.					
3. I produce brochures, packets, or pamphlets to highlight school programs, activities, student achievement.					
4. I have a parent handbook.					
5. I generate surveys for parent input or assessment.					
6. I respond in writing to parent concerns or criticisms.					
7. I send thank your notes.					
8. I write to parents recognizing their child's behavior and/or achievement.					
9. I send special purpose bulletins to inform parents of important issues and/or problems.					
10. I have a parent-teacher conference guide.					
11. I create flyers or posters to advertise school events.					
12. I provide parents a school calendar of events.					
13. I write letters of commendation.					
TOTAL YOUR YES/ NO/ DEL/ RESPONSES					

STUDENTS	NO	YES	DEL	DWM	QY
1. I have a student handbook.					
2. I publish a student newsletter.					
3. I write welcome letters to new students.					
4. I develop student surveys.					
5. I respond in writing to student questions or concerns.					
6. I send thank you notes to students.					
7. I send special occasion cards or notes.					
8. I produce recognition awards/ certificates.					
TOTAL YOUR YES/ NO/ DEL/ RESPONSES					

PEERS	NO	YES	DEL	DWM	QY
1. I use e-mail.					
2. I keep colleagues informed of school issues, achievements, and events.					
3. I send special occasion notes or cards.					
4. I submit proposals for participation in professional meetings, conferences, and programs.					
5. I recognize the achievements of peers in writing.					
6. I write articles for professional journals.					
TOTAL YOUR YES/NO/DEL/ RESPONSES					

CENTRAL OFFICE	NO	YES	DEL	DWM	QY
1. I write school improvement reports.					
2. I develop professional development plans.					
3. I have a school-community public relations plan.					
4. I complete required paperwork on time.					
5. I keep the superintendent informed.					
6. I use e-mail.					
7. I develop inservice workshops.					
8. I write grants.					
9. I produce annual reports.					
TOTAL YOUR YES/ NO/ DEL/ RESPONSES					

GENERAL COMMUNITY	NO	YES	DEL	DWM	QY
1. I write news releases.					
2. I write news articles about school events/staff/students.					
3. I design questionnaires to survey the local community about the school.					

1. I develop publicity brochures to highlight school programs and achievements.					
2. I respond in writing to questions, concerns, and rumors.					
3. I know the key opinion leaders in the community and keep them informed about important issues.					
4. I create posters and flyers to advertise school events.					
5. I have an Internet web page about my school.					
TOTAL YOUR YES/NO/ DEL/ RESPONSES					

Exercise 1.4
ANALYZING YOUR WRITING PATTERNS

What audiences do you write to most frequently? Are you neglecting a particular audience? Examine your communication methods and channels for each audience. Are you utilizing the variety of options available to you? Look at your contact frequency. Assess your timing of important information.

AUDIENCE	NO	YES	DELEGATED
Staff (16)			
Parents (13)			
Students (8)			
Peers (6)			
Central Office (9)			
General Community (8)			
TOTAL (60)			

Is there any relationship between and among the following areas?

Writing Apprehension Score
Low (20-39)   Moderate (40-68)   High (69-100)

Job Writing Frequency
High (41-60)   Moderate (20-40)   Low (0-20)

Effective Writing Behaviors
Always Do   Generally Do   Sometimes Do   Never Do

SUMMARY

The purpose of this chapter is to help you focus on your communication competence in the following areas:

♦ Your attitude toward writing.

♦ Your daily writing habits.

♦ Your communication patterns with your various audiences.

Exercise 1.5
MY COMMUNICATION PROFILE

Directions: Write what you have learned about yourself in each of these areas. What further information do you need?

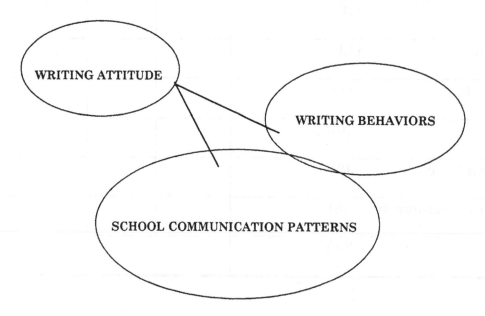

REFERENCES

Conrad, C. (1985). *Strategic organizational communication*. New York: Holt, Rinehart and Winston.

Daly, J. (1985). Writing apprehension. In Rose, M. (Ed.), *When a writer can't write* (pp. 43-82), New York: The Guilford Press.

Joyce, A. (1991). *Written communications and the school administrator*. Boston, MA: Allyn and Bacon.

Podsen I. (1987). *School administrators: The role of writing apprehension on job-related writing tasks and writing performance*. Unpublished Dissertation. Atlanta, GA: Georgia State University.

2

TARGETING CRITICAL WRITING DIMENSIONS

"Failure is not the worst thing in the world.
The very worst is not to try."
—NASSP Great Quotations

During the course of the day, administrators grapple with a multitude of writing tasks from short memos to lengthy school improvement reports. Each type of writing requires a specific approach in order to be effective. Before we explore these writing types, a brief overview of critical writing dimensions will establish a frame of reference as we navigate through the following chapters. Throughout this guide, we will center your attention on five critical writing dimensions:

- ◆ Your PURPOSE for writing
  (What do you want to happen? What do you want your reader to do, say, think, or perform?)

- ◆ Your AUDIENCE
  (Staff, parents, central office, peers, students, community)

- ◆ Your ORGANIZATIONAL strategy
  (Chronological Order, Topic Order, Need/Plan/Benefit, Problem/Solution, etc.)

- ◆ Your TONE
  (Collaborative, Authoritative, Complimentary, Objective, Friendly, Supportive)

- ◆ Your Writing FORM
  (What type of writing is needed and is most appropriate to accomplish my purpose?)

AUDIENCE AND PURPOSE

Before you even think about putting pen to paper or turning on the computer screen, be sure to ask yourself the two most important questions about any piece of correspondence: Who is my audience? and What is my purpose in writing to this audience?

WHO IS MY AUDIENCE?

What do I know about this audience that should influence any aspect of my writing? Have my previous experiences been positive, negative, or neutral? Have I established a history with this audience? Does this audience have any personal needs, interests, experiences, personal situations about which I should be aware and which should influence my approach to the situation?

In other words, it is important to take into consideration everything you already know about your audience and about your relationship to that audience before you begin to address the situation. When writing to many members of the staff, such knowledge and insight may come automatically to you because of your history with them. For others, you may need to think more consciously and carefully to identify those characteristics which you need to consider. Whatever the case, the important thing is to be certain you have identified your audience and that you have determined what you need to know to address that audience effectively.

WHAT IS MY PURPOSE IN WRITING TO THIS AUDIENCE?

Why am I writing to this audience? Addressing this question implies two considerations:

- ◆ Could my purpose be accomplished in some manner other than through writing? Could I walk down the hall and deliver the message verbally? Would that be a better way of conveying the message? Is it really necessary to write?

- ◆ Once I've determined that a written message is the proper mode of communication for this particular message, what do I hope to accomplish through this correspondence? Do I expect the audience to do something as a result? Do I simply want the audience to know something? What are the expectations that have caused me to write?

The failure to ask these two vital questions probably lies at the heart of most failed correspondence. When people don't ask these questions, they usually flounder and write aimlessly, often writing around and around the actual subject without ever coming to grips with it because they have not properly identified the subject for themselves.

The positive side of that coin is that when writers do ask these two questions, they provide the kind of focus and direction which allows them to write clearly, succinctly, and effectively. They know where they want to go and what they want to accomplish. Having identified these two goals, their writing often flows effortlessly and accomplishes what they expect.

If you are not already in the habit of very consciously identifying your *audience* and *purpose* before you begin writing, you might find it very helpful to start writing the two words right at the top of your memo pad or typing them right at the top of your computer screen before you begin every piece of writing for a while. Make it part of your writing routine. Then make sure you identify both characteristics as clearly as possible. You will soon find that doing so will make your writing flow more smoothly.

ORGANIZATIONAL STRATEGY

Once you have clearly identified your purpose and audience you are ready to begin drafting your ideas. The following chart outlines the various ways you can shape your message. Having an organizational strategy gives you a blueprint to follow in keeping your thoughts relevant and in logical sequence.

FIGURE 2.1. ORGANIZATIONAL TACTICS

TACTIC	DESCRIPTION
• Analytical Approach	State situation, your analysis, and conclusions.
• Chronological Approach	List the activities by order of time or sequence.
• Deductive Approach	Start with a summary of conclusions or recommendations; then support with facts and findings.

• Inductive Approach	Open with facts and findings; then present conclusions and/or recommendations. This approach is often used in "giving bad news."
• Need/Plan/Benefit	Begin with a description of the current need in your situation, outline a plan to meet the need, and then state the benefits.
• Problem/Solution	Disclose the dilemma; then offer your solution.
• Topic Approach	Identify the key points and then develop each one. Order of topics is by preference.
• Question/Answer	Raise the issue by asking a question; then answer it.

TONE

Be sure to adopt the right tone. If you have taken the time to consider all you know about your intended audience, you need to go the next step by doing all you can to establish the appropriate tone when addressing your topic with that audience. Your first consideration will certainly be to communicate your ideas in a professional tone. You are the principal. You are the chief teacher in your building. You must be sure to teach by example as well as by pronouncement.

STAY COOL AND CLARIFY YOUR THINKING

The language you use and the tone you establish will tell your audience much about you, about how you perceive the topic and how you feel about the audience. By keeping your tone entirely detached and level headed, no matter how frustrated or angry or put upon you might feel, you will have communicated your ability to rise above such considerations to keep the topic on a truly professional level.

If, however, you feel so frustrated or angry or put upon that you feel that you simply must put your ideas into writing, by all means do so. Writing out your anger or frustration will definitely help you clarify exactly what and how you feel about the situation. It is extremely therapeutic to vent yourself on the paper or screen. So go ahead; write it out. Write it all out. **Just don't send it.** Put it away and don't look at it for at least 24 hours. Then reread it to see whether or not you still feel the same way and whether or not you want that person to know you feel that way. If you still think you want to send it, ask another administrator or a trusted colleague or your mentor or your spouse to read it. Ask that person only to respond to how he or she would feel about receiving the correspondence. Chances are that somewhere along the line you will begin to modify, to soften, to lessen the harshness so that the document will have the proper professional tone for the educational leader of the building to communicate.

FIGURE 2.2. TAKING STOCK OF TONE

Pawlas and Meyers (1989) give us a framework to consider in judging our approach.

• Authoritative	This is threatening and cast in iron.
• Collaborative	This respects the expertise of others and encourages shared decision making.
• Complimentary	This gives someone a pat on the back.
• Supportive	This is constructive criticism with an offer of help.
• Informal/Friendly	This acknowledges ongoing professional respect and rapport.
• Objective	This just reports the facts directly and candidly.

FORM

In addition to these four aspects, we want to center your attention on FORM. Purpose and form deal with a wide range of possibilities available to you. The following table shows you how purpose and form are closely linked and provides you with a useful framework in developing any written communication document. Such a framework, when considered with an organizational strategy, your intended audience and tone should help you in creating effective written products.

FIGURE 2.3. WRITING FORMS

To Inform or Advise

Memos	Minutes of meetings
Business letters	Invitations

Newsletters	Programs
Brochures	e-mail
Flyers	Reports
Forms	Agendas
Posters	School Calendars
Brochures	Speeches
School Handbooks	

To Command or Direct

Memos/Letters requiring specific action	School Rules and Regulations for safety and health
Instructions	Letters of reprimand
Directions	e-mail
Policies and Procedures	

To Describe

Anecdotal records	Parent-Teacher conference guides
Teacher observation notes and scripts	Curriculum guides
Reports of a sequence of events	School newsletters
Professional development plans	News releases
Brochures on school programs	Articles for professional journals
Flyers	Articles for school newsletters

To Persuade

Letters of recommendation	Speeches
Editorials	Applications
Grant proposals	Resumes
Letters/Memos of request	Cover letters
Notes for a debate/meeting	

To Show Appreciation

Letters/Memos of commendation	Special occasion cards
Thank you notes	Staff-student-parent recognition awards

To Clarify Thinking

Note-taking	Mindmapping
Explanations	Outlines
Jottings of sensory impressions from observations, meetings, conferences	Visual/graphic organizers
Journals	

To Explore and Build Relationships

Questionnaires	Memos/Letters responding to problems/concerns/criticisms
Surveys	School-community public relations plans
Greeting cards	

To Make Comparisons

Charts	Descriptions
Tables	School Improvement Reports
Diagrams, graphs	Program Evaluation Reports

To Predict or Hypothesize

Speculations about probable outcomes in conclusions, recommendations, and development plans	Questions for meetings, conferences, interviews
Professional articles	Proposals

SUMMARY

The information in this chapter highlights the essential information you need in order to write more effectively. We will refer to these critical dimensions in the training modules that follow. Our purpose is to give you a short refresher course on those elements that will help you write more quickly.

REFERENCES

Pawlas, G., and Meyers, K. (1989). *The principal and communication.* Bloomington, IN: Elementary Principal Series No. 3. Phi Delta Kappa Educational Foundation.

3

SHARPENING YOUR WRITING SKILLS

"People forget how fast you did a job—
but they remember how well you did it."
—NASSP Great Quotations

Effective writing skills form the foundation for successful written communication. They are so basic that quite often we forget their significance. Chapter 1 of the guide asked you to assess your skills in several key topics. This chapter presents information in seven areas to help you master these skills.

WRITING CLEARLY AND CONCISELY

When administrators were asked, "What bugs you about your writing or the writing of other principals?" the majority describe such writing as "too long," or "it lacks clarity." This aspect is a major problem for most adult writers. If this is a problem area for you, use the following checklist to help you achieve more clarity and conciseness in your writing. Remember: *Failing to plan is planning to fail.*

♦ **Identify your purpose.** Why are you writing; what do you want to accomplish?

- **Think about your audience.** If you are writing to many, picture one person in that audience and write to that individual. Assess attitude and the amount of information needed.

- **List the key points and ideas you want to address.** Then highlight the points that support your purpose and meet the needs of your audience.

- **Write a first draft.** Next review it for explicitness and brevity. Check sentence length and paragraph construction. Sentences should run between 18-22 words; paragraphs should include 3 to 5 sentences on a single topic.

- **Read the document out loud.** What image do you want to project? What tone do you want to convey—helpful, apologetic, objective, caring, appreciative, formal, informal, humorous?

- **Get feedback from a trusted colleague on your writing.** Ask him or her specifically, "What is the message? What is the tone? What is not clear?" When your colleague's understanding of your ideas matches your purpose, then you will know your writing is becoming clear.

WRITING CORRECTLY:
GRAMMAR, SPELLING, PUNCTUATION

As principals we can't afford to let poor writing get past the school door. It will seriously impact on our professional credibility and the credibility of our school. Our school audiences expect, even demand, that we show a high degree of skill in the technical components of our language. If you are concerned about the basic elements of writing consider the following steps:

1. Ask your secretary to compile a list of your most common writing errors that he or she finds in your writing.

2. Find a grammar book that you can use as a reference tool in working on your precision in this area. Flag those sections that address your problem areas.

3. If you use a computer (and we think you should), obtain spell checking and grammar checking software programs to use with your writing. A good program can also teach you the rules you are breaking as it checks your work. However, don't assume these programs will catch everything.

4. Create an editing team to proofread all writing that leaves the school.

5. Model the way. Ask teachers to review your writing and encourage them to critique each other's writing. As the instructional leader you should be reviewing formal teacher letters to parents on a regular basis.

NOT USING EDUCATIONAL JARGON

Like most professionals in a specialized career, we develop buzz words and complex terminology unique to our working world. Memos and letters that contain these terms may seem very clear to those within our organization, but they are likely to confuse and frustrate individuals outside our school system.

When writing to a diverse group of individuals such as parents, keep the educationese to a minimum. Better yet, eliminate it. Use the following suggestions to help you determine the effective use of jargon.

   ♦ Analyze your audience. If you are writing to staff, the use of common jargon may be appropriate, even desirable. However, parents and professionals outside our school are more likely to be confused or misinterpret these words.

   ♦ If the term is unavoidable in a document, define the term or use the term in a context that clarifies its meaning.

ELIMINATING UNNECESSARY DETAIL

Part of the problem in writing clearly and concisely is knowing what information is essential and what information can be eliminated or packaged differently. If you follow the steps outlined in the section, *Writing Clearly and Concisely*, you will at least begin the process more efficiently. To help reduce eye strain and extraneous detail, try these suggestions.

   ♦ Before tackling a memo or report that includes a large amount of information, list the points or major recommendations you want to make. Summarize this information and then provide the supporting details in an addendum.

   ♦ When writing longer documents such as school improvement reports, ask the recipient of the document what information is critical and what can be eliminated.

   ♦ Organize the document with clear headings and subheadings. See if you can cover the content using fewer words.

WRITING WITH PIZZAZZ

Perhaps you feel pretty comfortable with your writing skill. None of these areas are troublesome for you. Then you might be ready to develop a style that's expressive and uniquely your own. This is the touch that compels your reader to keep reading. Consider these guidelines in developing a more interesting writing style.

- Avoid opening your sentences with overused phrases like "It is" and "There are" and "Thank you for your letter on" or " Per your request, please find the enclosed report on...." Yawn. Z...z...z...z... Grab attention quickly.

- Increase your vocabulary. Look for interesting and dynamic words in your personal and professional reading. Jot them down and check out their meaning. Try to use them in your writing when appropriate. Effective writers select words carefully to carry precise meaning and intended impressions.

- Give your sentences more punch. Use the active voice whenever possible. Use results-oriented action words such as *calculated, leveraged, restored, networked, formulated, detected, strategized*, etc. For example:

  PASSIVE VOICE
  Principals are energized by an enthusiastic staff.

  ACTIVE VOICE
  An enthusiastic staff energizes principals.

  The active verb "energizes" is stronger than the passive verb "are energized by." Sentences that reflect the active voice are usually shorter.

- Create visuals to help you illustrate a point and add impact to your writing documents. Computer technology gives you the power of the graphic designer at the touch of the mouse.

ALLOCATING WRITING TIME

If procrastination describes you when it comes to writing, think about setting aside a certain time each day for writing tasks. Breaking your "writing resistance" can start as simply as finding a time and place to write on a regular basis and organizing the writing task into smaller and more manageable blocks. For example, in attacking your in-basket consider the following suggestions:

- Read each in-basket item, sorting for priority and/or time deadlines.

- Decide which items can be handled by phone, face-to-face interaction, or delegated to a staff member.

- Choose which items can be handled by a note on the original.

- Use planning sheets for items requiring a written response to get you started quickly (see Figure 3.1). Duplicate these sheets and have them handy.

♦ Find a template that matches your writing needs and create your first draft.

FIGURE 3.1. ACTION PLANNING SHEET

What is my PURPOSE?
I expect to inform, describe, persuade, command, or show appreciation.

Who is my AUDIENCE? What is the attitude of my audience? Neutral, positive, hostile? What information does this audience need or is willing to accept?

What TONE do I want to convey? Collaborative, authoritative, complimentary, friendly, objective, or supportive?

What ORGANIZATIONAL STRATEGY should I use to shape my message? Topic approach, chronological order, need/plan/benefit, problem-solution, question/answer?

Getting started with a writing task will be easier if you set aside time to plan your writing strategy. By using planning sheets you begin to develop ways to use your time efficiently. When interruptions arise, and they will, you can return to the writing task more easily because you have designed a plan of attack.

COLLABORATING ON WRITING TASKS

Unlike Bill Bentley who took his writing tasks home, allocating a time for writing on the job also allows you to use your colleagues as writing coaches and peer editors. Learning to seek feedback on your writing does two things:

♦ You get help from a trusted peer or staff member immediately.

♦ You model the way for building collaboration on school writing tasks.

GETTING HELP

Are you taking advantage of your secretary's organizational skills? Joyce (1991) tells us that "because schools usually have a shortage of secretarial personnel, it is important to develop routines that utilize their assistance most effectively" (p. 14). She offers these suggestions:

♦ Let your secretary do the "preliminary sorting." Before you approach your in-basket, ask your secretary to organize your paperwork into specific packets. Work with your secretary in identifying how you want the information sorted. Here's a start:

Signature Only

Routine Memos and Letters/Not Urgent

Special Memos and Letters/Urgent

General Information Announcements/Important but Not Urgent

Professional Catalogues and Journals

Upcoming Deadlines for Reports or Projects

♦ Develop a template file of memos and letters that address typical requests and concerns from parents, staff, and the general community. Ask your secretary to read through the routine memos and letters and develop a draft by pulling up a similar request from your template file, updating and revising it, and then attaching it to the current correspondence. All you have to do is review the draft, make any changes, and return it to your secretary for final printing.

The key here is organizing your correspondence files so that you or your secretary can find previous memos, letters or reports quickly. Again, work with your secretarial staff so you are all on the same page. Develop a system that works and saves everybody time. Don't assume your secretary will do these things or organize incoming paperwork the way you would do it. Part of your job is working with your office staff in contriving a system that is best for you AND your office.

MODELING THE WAY

Asking for help or feedback on your writing tasks is not an easy thing to do. After all as the *principal teacher* in the school you are expected to know how to write. Right? Well, let's see if we can approach this from a different angle. Chances are your staff is critiquing your writing style in some fashion already. Have you ever found one of *your* memos pinned to the staff bulletin board with red ink circling a writing error? *Not a pretty sight!* Why not take advantage of it? Put your cards on the table. Tell your staff you are working on your writing and would like their help. As a matter of fact you encourage all your teachers to share their written correspondence with one another to make sure only *perfect* writing gets past the school door.

Now instead of an adversarial relationship on this issue you start a process for helping others to collaborate with you in developing sensitive and effective school-home communication correspondence. When asking for feedback, be specific about the information you are seeking.

Exercise 3.1
YOUR EDITING CHECKLIST

This checklist may provide a strategy to use in checking the basic features of your writing. Select one or two of your writing products and use this checklist to assess your writing. Ask a colleague (preferably one of your English teachers) to critique the same writing documents. What are your strength areas? What are your growth targets?

Organization

I have identified my purpose.
I have assessed my audience.
I have stated my main points clearly.
I have enough details to support my purpose.
I have organized the content logically/sequentially.
I have used effective transitions.

Sentence Structure

My sentence length is between 18 and 20 words.
I have used the active voice.
I have no sentence fragments or run-ons.
My paragraphs include a variety of sentence types.
    (Simple, compound, and complex)
The sentences have clear subjects and verbs.

Grammatical Errors

The verbs agree with their subjects.
The pronouns have clear antecedents.
I have not used an adjective in place of an adverb.
None of my modifiers are misplaced.
I have made no shifts in tense.

Word Choice

I have used action-oriented verbs.
I have avoided words with negative connotations.
I have omitted unnecessary words and expressions.
I have avoided clichés and educational jargon.
I have chosen words that say exactly what I mean.
My sentences do not begin with overused phrases.
My writing conveys my intended tone.

Mechanics

No words are misspelled.
I have eliminated unnecessary commas.
I have not used unnecessary quotation marks or exclamation points.

I have made any abbreviations clear.

I have not accidentally omitted a word or sentence.

My document looks professional.

I have used headings and subheadings.

I have varied the font style and size.

I have utilized the computer to enhance my written documents.

SUMMARY AND TIPS

Remember these three writing principles offered by Joyce Wycoff (1991):

First and foremost: No one wants to read it!

Second and important: Almost no one will read all of it!

Third and critical: Almost everyone will misunderstand some part of it (p. 69). Therefore,

♦ Keep sentences and paragraphs short.

♦ Write like you speak to make your writing more readable.

♦ Plan your written documents before beginning to write.

♦ Consider your audience and its needs.

♦ Edit and proofread all your correspondence for common errors.

♦ Use a variety of sentence openers and sentence structures.

♦ Eliminate the use of jargon.

♦ Increase your vocabulary.

♦ Use charts, tables, and graphics to reinforce your message.

♦ Allocate time for writing.

♦ Seek feedback on your writing.

REFERENCES

Joyce, A. (1991). *Written communications and the school administrator.* Boston, MA: Allyn and Bacon.

Wycoff, J. (1991). *Mindmapping.* New York: Berkley Books.

PART TWO

TRAINING MODULES

COMPETENCY ONE

MEMOS

COMPETENCY STATEMENT

Write skillfully developed memos to build effective internal written communication channels within the school community.

KNOWLEDGE BASE HIGHLIGHTS

Hennington 1978. The memo saves valuable managerial time. It can simplify correspondence procedures and improve communication by transmitting written information rapidly and conveniently between members of an organization.

Roddick 1986. You will sharpen your competitive edge by increasing the effectiveness of your writing skills. Clear and persuasive memos will make a good impression on your professional colleagues.

Joyce 1991. "Although effective verbal communication skills are almost prerequisite to becoming a school administrator, once appointed to the position, a principal or assistant principal quickly realizes the necessity for good letter writing skills."

Yerkes & Morgan 1991. "Memos are compact communications intended to trigger action."

Drake & Roe 1994. "Frequency is not as important as clarity of purpose and clarity of the message in your written communication."

Johnston 1994. Many administrators routinely send imperious, ineffective memoranda without realizing how their messages sound. Good professional talk requires:

awareness of tone, planning ahead the needed information, and attention to the details that will help make the message more palatable to the receiver.

MEMOS TRIGGER ACTION

Principals communicate in writing most often to internal audiences such as staff and central office personnel; therefore, memos and letters are the most utilized forms of written communication. Communication by memorandum saves valuable managerial time. The effective administrator knows when and how to use this communication tool to simplify correspondence procedures and to expedite the flow of information between and among members of the school system.

> DATE: September 20, _____
> TO: Our Colleagues in the Trenches
> FROM: The Authors
> SUBJECT: Memo Writing Tips

- **"Memos are a quick call to action.** Be sure the reader understands what you want and when you want it."￼ As the memo writer, you may need to give information concerning new policies and staff decisions, relay asked-for information, present facts for decision making by others, report progress on school projects, suggest ideas, justify or set responsibility for certain courses of action, or take a stand on an issue. Memos are useful in making sure that information communicated verbally is not forgotten or misunderstood.

- **"Memos can go up, down, or across the organizational structure.** It's all right to send a memo to the boss." Memos are internal business communications. The effective principal keeps the superintendent informed and up to date on pertinent issues. More important, the effective school leader knows that internal communication cannot be left to chance. Both upward and downward communication channels must be planned and utilized. Generally, letters are used when writing to people outside the organization.

- **A memo is an effective method to express appreciation and build esprit de corps within the school.** A short memo to a teacher who has performed an outstanding lesson often has a greater effect than a verbal compliment. Memos acknowledging how staff members have contributed to the school's functioning not only benefits working relationships but also shows that you, as the school leader, have one of the qualities of an effective administrator, the ability to recognize exceptional performance.

- **The most important part of the memo is the body.** Memos emphasize the important facts, avoiding needless and trivial details. Get to the point quickly by using short words, sentences, paragraphs, and lists to keep the reader's interest.

♦ **Effective memo writers include at least three parts in their memos:**

Introduction: State the purpose of the memo and the method used to obtain information presented.

Body: Assert the message objectively and include sufficient detailed information. Avoid mixing opinion with facts in this part of the memo.

Conclusion: Summarize the facts, outline a plan of action or make recommendations for future action. "Personal comments and opinions may be included in this section; however, conclusions must be supported by facts or other evidence presented in the memo" (Hennington, p. 86).

♦ **Effective memo writers choose an organizational strategy that best suits their purpose.** No rigid rules govern the content and organization of memos. Here are the most frequently used organizational tactics found in businesslike writing.

TACTIC	DESCRIPTION
• Analytical Approach	State situation, your analysis, and conclusions.
• Chronological Approach	List the activities by order of time or sequence.
• Deductive Approach	Start with a summary of conclusions or recommendations; then support with facts and findings.
• Inductive Approach	Open with facts and findings; then present conclusions and/or recommendations. This approach is often used in "giving bad news."
• Need/Plan/Benefit	Begin with a description of the current need in your situation, outline a plan to meet the need, and then state the benefits.
• Problem/Solution	Disclose the dilemma; then offer your solution.
• Topic Approach	Identify the key points and then develop each one. Order of topics is by preference.
• Question/Answer	Raise the issue by asking a question; then answer it.

♦ **"Keep your audience, not the directive or information, in mind."** Before beginning to write a memo, you should complete this sentence:

I want (WHO) to do (WHAT) because (REASON).

If you can't complete this sentence you need to REEXAMINE your audience and your purpose for writing this memo.

♦ **Know the ten parts to an effective memo:**

MEMORANDUM Head	The word **MEMORANDUM** printed in capital letters at top of paper.
TO Line:	Identifies the memo recipient.
FROM Line:	Identifies the writer.
Writer's Initials	Memo writer's initials by the typed name on *FROM LINE*.
DATE Line	For both reference and legal reasons, all memos should be dated.
RE: Subject Line or Action Requested Line	Announces the topic of memo; provides a useful way to file and retrieve correspondence.
Body	Contains the message.
Reference Initials	Reflects the initials of the secretary who prepared the memo.
Enc.,Encl.,Enc.1 Enclosure Notation	Used if one or more items are included with the memo. Include the title of the enclosure.
cc: Carbon Copy Notation	Indicates a copy has been directed to another person.

- ◆ **"Make it easy for the reader to take action."** Consider adding a contact line: Ex: "Contact: Call Mr. Glenn Jones in Personnel at extension 381."

- ◆ **"Add a response line at the end of the memo."** The reader can jot down his or her reply for a prompt response.

- ◆ **Develop a variety of printed memo formats.** Your computer software program usually has formatted templates ready to use.

Adapted from Yerkes & Morgan (1991). *Strategies for Success: An Administrator's Guide to Writing.* NASSP: Reston, VA. pp. 16-17. Boldface quotations are cited directly from this source.

Adapted from Hennington (1978). "Memorandums—An Effective Communication Tool for Managers." In *Business Communication* by Golen, Figgins, and Smeltzer (1984). New York: John Wiley and Sons, pp. 82-89.

Here's a sample memo written by a colleague. We think it represents an effective memo. What do you think?

TEMPLATE C1-1. MEMO TO STAFF
PURPOSE: TO PERSUADE
AUDIENCE: TEACHING STAFF
TONE: SUPPORTIVE
STRATEGY: NEED/PLAN/BENEFIT

MEMORANDUM   **Document Analysis**

TO: Teaching Staff
FROM: E.S. Principal
RE: Teacher Evaluation
DATE: September 12, ___

The philosophy and purpose of teacher evaluation is to focus our attention on teaching and learning in our school. The process should provide valuable information for us to use in developing the best learning environment for our students; in addition, it should also create a climate that stimulates our own professional growth. The bottom line is, always will be, how staff impacts on our students' well-being and educational progress.	Introduces the topic. Describes the current need.
One of our district goals developed jointly by the two building teams is to explore alternative assessment methods for both students and teachers. I would like to begin this process with an alternative assessment sug-	Outlines the plan.

gestion for our teacher evaluation program. The Teacher Portfolio Assessment is not a cumbersome process and allows a lot of flexibility in its format and design.

Take some time to review the attached overview of this type of assessment. Think about it, ask questions, and decide if you would like to experiment with it. This is not mandatory; it is strictly voluntary on your part. If you would like to give it a try, work on the goals section and then set up an initial meeting with me to begin the process. I would like to have the initial meetings completed by the second week in October. If you decide this assessment process is not for you, you will be evaluated in the same manner used last year.

Provides the supporting details in an addendum.

I hope that many of you will take advantage of this new format. This self-directed goal-setting approach to teacher evaluation is fairly new, but research indicates that teachers find it personally rewarding and professionally meaningful—something we all hope to find during our careers. Specifically, I believe it will benefit you in three ways:

Summarizes the benefits of plan.

Uses the active voice.

Keeps sentences short and clear.

1. Allows the teacher to identify and set targeted goals based on individual needs, skills, and experiences;

Uses a listing format.

2. Provides flexibility in collecting and reviewing data to support goal achievement;

3. Empowers teachers to take charge of their professional development.

Please let me know your intentions by September 20th so that I can begin my planning and scheduling process.

Indicates action requested.

ES/sf

Reference initials.

Encl. 1: Teacher Portfolio Overview

Enclosure notation.

Before and After Memos

What follows are several disguised versions of *real* memos written by our well-intentioned colleagues. Glance at the "before" version and respond to the instructions in the column marked "Document Analysis." Then glance at the "after" version on the opposite side of the page. Review the "Document Analysis" column for the changes we made.

MEMORANDUM

October 15,____

TO: All Staff Members
FR: Martha Murphy
RE: Staff Inservice

Our school system is facing rapidly changing student and community demographics. Quite often teachers are not kept informed of these changes and the possible consequences for teaching and learning in their classrooms. Many teachers have expressed concerns about the rising rate of school misbehavior, suspensions, and school-related violence.

The staff development department wants to bridge this communication gap by updating teachers on the changing student and community demographics in our school system and the implications for teachers.

The logical step is a workshop that addresses these issues. Dr. Discipline, a noted teacher educator, will present his views on classroom management as it relates to changing school populations on Friday, November 10, from 4 until 6 p.m. at the Staff Development Center.

We would hope that after attending this workshop you could return to your classroom with a better understanding of your students' needs and several alternative approaches in managing students' behavior.

This inservice will be beneficial to all teachers. We all have the same goal of reaching and teaching all students. We hope the exchange of ideas will foster this objective. We look forward to seeing you on November 10.

Document Analysis

Principals are busy people but so are staff members.

What is it like to get a memo that must be read several times in order to figure out what the writer wants?

Let's examine this memo. Underline the reason or purpose of this memo. Is there more than one?

Draw a line to the part of the memo that answers the Five W's.

WHO

WHAT

WHEN

WHERE

WHY

How clear is the message?

Check sentence length.

TEMPLATE C1-2. AFTER
PURPOSE: TO INFORM/ANNOUNCE
AUDIENCE: STAFF
TONE: COLLABORATIVE
STRATEGY: FIVE W'S

MEMORANDUM	**Document Analysis**
	Tells the readers what they need to know up front.
October 15, ____	
TO: Staff Members FR: Martha Murphy RE: Teacher Workshop	
FULTON COUNTY STAFF DEVELOPMENT DEPARTMENT	Who
INVITES YOU TO A CLASSROOM MANAGEMENT WORKSHOP	What
with **Dr. Discipline**	
Friday, November 10 **4 to 6 P.M.**	When
Fulton County Staff Development Center	Where
◆ Why am I experiencing more student misbehavior in my classroom?	Why
◆ What effect does changing demographics have on my school and its local community?	Relates the workshop to the reader's needs. Uses summary statements and bullets to highlight.
◆ How can I incorporate additional behavior management strategies into my overall classroom management plan?	
Tune in Friday, November 10, and learn how we can all work together to develop our classroom management skills. Discover how different ethnic and cultural groups respond to various discipline approaches. Then give us your feedback, questions, and suggestions for other in-service programs.	Summarizes the message. Keeps sentences between 18-20 words.
We look forward to your participation.	

MEMORANDUM

TO: State Visiting Team Members
FR: Dan Polite, Principal
RE: Hospitality Arrangements and Schedule

Welcome and thank you for agreeing to serve on our interim self-study visit. We are looking forward to working with you this week. Hopefully you have had no trouble with travel arrangements or hotel accommodations.

We will be starting tomorrow morning with a continental breakfast at 7:30 in my conference room for the week. The classroom observations and meetings will begin at 8:30. You will be picked up at 7:00 by a staff member who will bring you to the school and return you in the evening.

The school system has arranged for master billing of your hotel room for the week, excluding telephone and any incidentals. Meals will be reimbursed.

On Wednesday evening, October 7, we are hosting a staff reception for the visiting team at the Pine Valley Golf Club from 6:00-7:00 p.m. Then the visiting team and hospitality committee will have dinner after the staff reception.

Again, welcome to our school. We are looking forward to meeting with you on Monday morning and to working with you throughout the week. Our teachers and students have worked hard in preparing for your visit.

Document Analysis

Put yourself in the reader's shoes. You are traveling to a strange city for a week-long school visitation.

What questions would you like answered?

Jot them down.

Now put a check next to each question that was answered in this response.

What questions are left unanswered?

How many scheduled events are mentioned in this memo?

TEMPLATE C1-3. AFTER
PURPOSE: TO INFORM
AUDIENCE: PEER
TONE: OBJECTIVE
STRATEGY: TOPIC ORDER/CHRONOLOGICAL

MEMORANDUM

Document Analysis

TO: State Visiting Team Committee Members
FR: Dan Polite, Principal
RE: Schedule and Hospitality Arrangements

Welcome to Springville and thank you for taking time
to serve on our Interim Self-Study Visit. We are looking
forward to working with you this week. Our teachers
and students have worked hard in preparing for your
visit.

Schedule Highlights

Monday to Friday, October 5-9

A timetable of events appears under the topic "Schedule Highlights."

♦ 7:30 a.m.   Continental breakfast in principal's conference room.

♦ 8:30 a.m.   Class visitations and meetings with staff, parents, and students.

♦ 5:00 p.m.   Return to hotel.

Wednesday, October 7

♦ 6:00 p.m.   Staff reception at the Pine Valley Golf Club, prior to:

♦ 7:30 p.m.   Dinner with selected staff members and school superintendent.

Expenses: The master billing for the Springville School
System includes your room and meals. Meals need to
stay within the state guidelines of $30 per day. The master bill will not include telephone calls and personal incidentals. Please keep receipts for any reimbursable expenses not included on the hotel bill.

Three other topics are emphasized. Each paragraph keeps to the topic and provides needed details.

Travel Arrangements: Staff members will pick you up
daily at 7:00 a.m. and return you to the hotel each afternoon at 5:00 p.m. On Wednesday, October 7, the staff
drivers will return you to the hotel to freshen up and re-

Information is easy to find. Highlighting the topics of the memo allows the reader to scan quickly.

main at the hotel. At 5:30 they will bring you to the Pine Valley Golf Club.

Need Help? Have a Question? We are looking forward to meeting you on Monday morning and to working with you on this project. If you should have questions or concerns, please call Angie Davis, the hospitality chair, at 770-345-7879.

Provides a contact number to call if problems occur.

BEFORE

MEMORANDUM

TO: Ms. Tardy
FR: Ms. Lane
RE: Classroom Supervision

This morning I visited your sixth grade classroom and found the students yelling and throwing books across the room. Two boys were pushing one another and one girl was standing in front of the room making obscene gestures. You were not in your classroom at 8:30 a.m. and did not arrive until 8:40 a.m.

One of two reasons for this unacceptable situation must be applicable: Either you do not care about the safety of the students or you have chosen to ignore your duties and responsibilities in this matter.

In an era of public distrust toward schools, we cannot afford to have students injure themselves due to teacher negligence. I will not tolerate any lack of buy in on anyone's part to our school goal of building community support.

Effective immediately, leaving your students unattended without notification to me or the assistant principal must result in immediate disciplinary action in accordance with county policies: verbal warning for first offense, written warning for second offense, probation for third, and recommendation for termination for the fourth.

Document Analysis

Giving "bad news" to staff members is never an easy task. To be useful, such a memo should result in corrective action.

If you were Ms. Tardy how might you react to this memo?

Memos such as this one may make the writer feel good but what effect does it have on the reader?

We suspect that as the teacher you might feel angry enough to quit or devastated enough to lose morale for teaching.

Let's assume this is not an ongoing problem situation.

Here's the rewrite.

Template C1-4. After
Purpose: To Reprimand
Audience: Teacher
Tone: Authoritative
Strategy: Problem-Solution

MEMORANDUM	**Document Analysis**

TO: Ms. Tardy
FR: Ms. Lane
RE: Classroom Supervision

Problem Situation: There is an urgent problem that needs your immediate attention: lack of teacher supervision in your first period class.

> States the purpose of the memo and what needs to change. Gains reader's attention fast!

I need to know if there are any extenuating circumstances that caused you to leave your class unattended for ten minutes today at the beginning of first period. I am counting on you to follow school policy about leaving students unsupervised. This is both policy, and more important, a top priority for student safety.

> Seeks additional information. Gives teacher chance to explain.
>
> Gives reasons for action taken.

Background: This morning I visited your sixth grade classroom and found the students yelling and throwing books across the room. Two boys were pushing one another and one girl was standing in front of the room making obscene gestures. You were not in your classroom at 8:30 a.m. and did not arrive until 8:40 a.m.

> Provides objective description of the incident.
>
> Sarcastic statements are deleted: "Either you do not care or..."

Action Required:

♦ Do not leave your students unattended at any time.

♦ Notify the office if you need to leave the room so we can cover your class.

> Indicates the desired behavior. Focus is on results and problem solving.

♦ Develop a plan on what steps you have taken and what help you need to see that this never happens again.

> Offers assistance.

Be ready to discuss this incident with me tomorrow at 8:00 a.m. in my office. I'm confident you can resolve this so that official disciplinary warnings will not become necessary.

> Describes future consequences. Offers support.

Exercise C1-1
IT'S YOUR TURN

Browse through your in-basket and select an item that you decide requires a written response. Follow these steps in preparing the memo.

♦ Complete the Action Planning Sheet and note your starting time in beginning this writing task.

Action Planning Sheet

Starting Time:_____

What is my purpose in writing this memo?

Who is my audience?

What is the attitude of this audience? Positive/Neutral/Negative?

What information do they need?

What tone do I want to convey?

♦ Map your ideas before you write. You can make a list, an outline, or a mindmap. The point is to put all your ideas down on paper. Let's try a listing format this time.

Getting Started

Once you have targeted your purpose and audience, list all your ideas by answering the following questions. Do not edit or evaluate. Just get all your ideas down on paper.

- WHO

- WHAT

- WHERE

- WHEN

- WHY

- HOW

♦ Select an organizational strategy. Refer to page 17 which outlines the ways you can structure the message. Which one will you use? If possible select a strategy that has been used in one of the "after" formats so you will have a visual example to model.

♦ Now draft your memo. Insert your disk and open file C1-5. Copy the template and write your memo.

TEMPLATE GUIDE C1-5
PURPOSE: TO_____
AUDIENCE: _____
TONE: _____
STRATEGY: _____

MEMORANDUM

Document Guide

DATE: _____

TO: _____

FROM: _____

RE: _____

_____

_____

_____

_____

Begin your Memo by:
♦ Getting your reader's attention.
♦ Telling the purpose.

_____

_____

_____

_____

_____

Develop your Memo by:
♦ Following an organizational strategy.
♦ Keeping paragraphs short (3-5 sentences on one topic).
♦ Using short sentences (18-21 words).

_____

_____

_____

_____

Conclude your Memo by:
♦ Emphasizing major points and/or
♦ Giving conclusions or recommendations.

- Edit your memo for sentence clarity, word choice, grammar, punctuation, word count, and spelling. Assess the tone. Use your computer's capability to help monitor these aspects of your writing.

- Make your memo visually appealing by varying font size, highlighting, or underlining. Use graphics when appropriate. Use your computer software program to help you format your memo; you may even have format template wizards to choose from on your system. Take the time now to experiment and find the look that suits your purpose and audience.

- Make revisions and seek feedback on clarity and success in communicating your purpose. Note your completion time.

- Save your memo for future reference. Add it to the disk and start expanding your template resource file.

Summary

Principals are incredibly busy people. Probably no one in the school system is more overburdened than the building administrators. Their tasks are myriad and diverse. They are constantly on center stage. Everything they say, do, and write is observed, reacted to, and scrutinized by their public.

While their actions and statements are always subject to public response and analysis, only their written words will remain for observation after the situation is over. Letters, memos, evaluations, and other written documents become part of a very public record. Principals need to do all they can to guarantee that they have done all they can to prevent their writing from coming back to haunt them at a later time. Principals cannot avoid writing, so they must make sure that their writing will present them in the best possible light. Writing clearly, simply, concisely, and correctly should enable the principal to communicate with authority, humanity, and pride.

References

Drake, T., and Roe, W. (1994). *The principalship* (4th ed.). New York: Macmillan.

Hennington, J. (1978). Memorandums—An effective communication tool for management. In *Business communication*, Golen, S., Figgins, R., and Smeltzer, L. (Eds.). New York: John Wiley & Sons, pp. 82-89.

Johnston, C. (August, 1994). Professional talk. *The Executive Educator, 16* (8), 40-41.

Joyce, A. (1991). *Written communications and the school administrator*. Boston, MA: Allyn and Bacon.

Roddick, E. (1986). *Writing that means business*. New York: Macmillan.

Yerkes, D., and Morgan, S. (1991). *Strategies for success: An administrator's guide to writing.* Reston, VA: National Association of Secondary School Principals.

COMPETENCY TWO

BUSINESS LETTERS

COMPETENCY STATEMENT

Develop dynamic business letters to promote positive and credible school-community written communication channels.

KNOWLEDGE BASE HIGHLIGHTS

Forbes 1981. "It's totally asinine to blow your chances of getting whatever you want with a business letter that turns people off instead of turning them on."

Watkins 1982. "Business has recognized the problem of bad writing and is emphasizing to its executives the importance of well-written memos and letters. Recognition of this problem is the first step toward a solution."

Roddick 1986. Each day on your job you are called upon to speak and write. Remember "when you open your mouth or write a letter or report, you will be advertising your progress and your potential worth." Both your internal and external public will form impressions of you based on your communication skills.

Joyce 1991. "A good letter can be an effective public relations tool; a poorly written letter can be a minor disaster."

Minninger 1992. "Perfect letters are not only good business, they may mean the difference between business and no business."

Letters That Mean Business

Principals write business letters to both internal and external audiences. A good business letter is a "get-ahead tool," according to Joan Minninger in her book, *The Perfect Letter*. She asserts that "better business starts with better communication."

In today's world school leaders who can prove they are results-oriented and show instructional gains to their school publics are supported. Principals who can handle correspondence in a timely manner and know how to say the right thing to a targeted audience build credibility and trust. It's the chance of exposure—of not knowing how to say the right thing or writing fear—that immobilizes the reluctant writer. Procrastination sets in, often resulting in little or no communication. Lack of communication as well as poor communication may be the difference between career advancement or working elsewhere.

Here's a real letter (disguised) sent to a state educational agency requesting information:

P.O. Box 1234
Trenton GA 30752
United States of America
May 3, 1995

Dear sirs:

       RE: Resources for mentoring

We at Crestwood Middle School in Trenton Georgia are contemplating

commencing the One-at-a-Time mentoring program and would appreciate very much if you would send us details of your resources. Many thanks.

Yours truly,

John Smith

The writer of this message does not create a positive and credible professional image of himself or the school. The cost of weak writing is high. According to Malcolm Forbes (*Forbes* Magazine), a good business letter can get you money, get help, or "get you off the hook." He offers these suggestions to get the job done right.

KNOW WHAT YOU WANT

- Write down your purpose in one sentence.

- List the major points before you write. Answer the 5 W's (Who, What, Where, When, and Why) or develop a mindmap to help organize ideas.

- If responding to a letter, check the points that need attention. Keep it in front of you to avoid omitting a pertinent issue or concern.

- Answer promptly.

JUMP RIGHT IN

- Call the reader by name, not "Dear Sir, Madame, or Ms."

- State the purpose in the first paragraph.

- Write the letter from the reader's point of view. Tell what's in it for him or her. Anticipate questions and objections.

- Create a positive impression even if you're delivering bad news. A real PR challenge!

- Write the way you speak. How many times have you started a conversation with "Thank you for your letter dated...?" Never, we would guess. Be specific, clear, and concise. Keep your letter to one page.

- "Lean heavier on nouns and verbs, lighter on adjectives. Use the active voice instead of passive" (Forbes, p. 80).

CHECK FOR VITAL BODY PARTS

- **The Inside Address.** Be a bean counter. When you write a business letter include the inside address, see that it's correct and complete. Sloppiness and inattention to detail are not characteristics of effective leaders.

- **The Date.** Two forms are acceptable. No date is unacceptable. For both reference and legal reasons, all your correspondence should be dated.

February 4, 1996 or
4 February 1996

♦ **Subject Line or Filing Reference.** A subject or reference line keeps you and the reader focused on the purpose of the letter. It also provides a handy cross-reference tool for filing all correspondence.

♦ **Salutation.** Select a greeting that reflects the formality of the message and the relationship you have to the reader. For example:

Hi! Joan,	Suggests something informal and chatty with a peer or staff member.
Dear Joan,	Suggests something more businesslike and routine to someone you know on a first-name basis.
Dear Joan:	Suggests something more formal and serious because it ends in a colon.
Dear Ms. Wilder:	Suggests something businesslike to someone you don't know on a first-name basis or the purpose of the message is very serious and requires a more formal greeting.
Dear Joan Wilder:	Not often used but is perfectly acceptable. Consider using when you don't know the reader well or know only by reputation.

♦ **The Message.** Organization is the key to success. Like the memo, the body of the letter should be clearly organized into three parts:

Introduction: State the purpose of the letter and the method used to obtain information presented.

Body: Assert the message objectively and include sufficient detailed information. Avoid mixing opinion with facts in this part of the letter.

Conclusion: Summarize the facts, outline a plan of action or make recommendations for future action. Support conclusions and recommendations with facts presented in the letter.

♦ **Business letters require clear reasoning and an orderly presentation of facts and ideas.** Use the organizational strategies on pages 17-18 to select the best way to structure your message. Letters are extensions of yourselves and your schools. They represent you to your various publics; a part of you is exposed and fixed in print. A snapshot, so to speak, of your thinking processes and writing skills for the world to see. This is a scary thought for many reluctant writers who find it difficult to convey the intended message.

♦ **The Closing and Signature.** Try to match the sign-off to the purpose and tone of the letter. Obviously, a letter of reprimand signed "Warmly," could be grounds for harassment. Check out your closings in your letters. How varied are they, or do you use the same one most of the time? How predictable of you! Try some of these. Can you think of others? List them on this page for quick reference.

> All the best,
> Best regards,
> Cordially,
> Cordially yours,
> Fondly,
> Regards,
> Regretfully,
> Respectfully,
> Sincerely,
> Sincerely yours,
> Thank you,
> Thinking of you,
> Very best regards,
> Very truly yours,
> Warmly,
> With sincere regrets,
> Yours truly,

GIVE IT YOUR BEST SHOT

♦ Use your computer technology to make your letter a real attention getter. Use headings to identify key sections or points. **Experiment with various fonts** to make your letter appealing and easy to read. <u>Underline important words or ideas</u> for emphasis. Failure to produce visually appealing and easy-to-read documents will put your letter (and your problem) at the bottom of your reader's *To Do List*!

♦ "Make it perfect. No typos, no misspellings, no factual errors" (Forbes, p. 80). Remember, this message represents you and your school.

♦ Don't be pretentious, Mr. or Ms. Know It All.

♦ Don't exaggerate.

♦ Be honest, direct, and cordial.

♦ Edit critically. Read your letter out loud.

♦ Get feedback from a colleague.

Adapted from Malcolm Forbes (1981). "How to Write a Business Letter." In *Business Communication* by Golen, Figgins, and Smeltzer (1984). John Wiley & Sons, New York, pp. 78-81.

Adapted from Ellen Roddick (1986). "Letters and Memos That Engage Readers." In *Writing That Means Business*, Macmillan, New York, pp. 36-49.

Here's a letter of recommendation written by a high school principal. We think it reflects the ideas outlined above. What do you think?

TEMPLATE C2-1. LETTER OF RECOMMENDATION
PURPOSE: TO RECOMMEND
AUDIENCE: PEER
TONE: COMPLIMENTARY
STRATEGY: INDUCTIVE/TOPIC APPROACH

Document Analysis

May 9, ___

Date line.

Mr. John Jackson, Principal
Fanning City High School
25 Sky Lane
Denver, CO 23567

Inside address.

SUBJECT: Letter of recommendation for Mr. Dan Owen.

Subject line.

Dear Mr. Jackson:

Formal greeting.

Mr. Dan Owen has asked me to write a letter of recommendation concerning his application for a teaching position in your social studies department.

First paragraph states the purpose.

Background Information:
Dan Owen was hired in the spring of 1993 as a permanent substitute in social studies for an indefinite period. While we made a commitment to him through the end of June, it was made clear that we didn't know when or if the teacher he was replacing would return. Since the bulk of his teaching schedule terminated in a Global Studies Regents, we were highly concerned

Uses headings to let the reader scan for information.

Summarizes background information concerning hiring circumstances.

about the students' preparation for these difficult exams. As a result of his conscientious efforts and the confidence he inspired in the students, the students completed the year on a very positive note with more than 80% passing the Regents exam.

Praises teacher and stresses results.

Having observed Mr. Owen in a very difficult set of circumstances and knowing that both students and parents were very pleased with his ability to motivate the reluctant learner, we hired Mr. Owen for a full-time tenured track position when we had the opportunity during the following fall.

Credentials:
Mr. Owen's training and preparation are largely in American History. He has been teaching both Regents and non-Regents eleventh graders over the past two school years. However, wishing to expand his background and make himself more flexible, he requested to teach ninth grade Global Studies on both the Regents and non-Regents level. To his credit, he has expended an inordinate amount of time in order to develop his own expertise in non-Western history. His lesson plans are detailed and include activities that are thought-provoking and require cooperative learning efforts.

Provides specific details regarding teaching background and subjects taught.

Points out teacher's initiative to expand knowledge base.

Points out instructional strengths.

Professional Recommendation:
Dan Owen is an asset to our Social Studies Department and I will regret losing him. He is young and responsive to constructive criticism. He is hard-working and relates to young adults in an extremely positive manner. His classes are interesting and his students truly enjoy them. During his two and a half years, he demonstrated high skill in classroom management. I am sure he will make the same positive contribution to your high school as he has to mine.

Ends with strong recommendation.

Summarizes teaching skills and professional qualities.

Sentences are short and clear.

Sincerely,

Closing.

Margaret Mills, Ph.D.
Principal

Signature.

MM/dh

Reference Initials.

Before and After Letters

What follows are several disguised versions of *real* letters written by our well-intentioned colleagues. Glance at the "before" version and respond to the instructions in the column marked "Document Analysis." Then glance at the "after" version on the opposite side of the page. Review the "Document Analysis" column for the changes we made.

Before

January 26, _____

Mr. Pete Smith
Cherokee Fencing Company
PO Box 100
Detroit, MI 30032

Dear Mr. Smith:

On Wednesday, January 12, 1996, it was noted by a staff member that the new fence around the primary recreational area was in need of repair. I contacted you by phone on January 13 and then again on January 20, regarding this matter.

You stated in our phone conversation that you would send a crew to repair the fence within one week. As discussed in our telephone conversation of January 13, it is our opinion that the fence should be repaired as soon as possible. As I explained to you, the two support posts were pulled out of the ground and the children in the primary grades could gain access to a very busy thoroughfare should they pull or push it over.

We hope you will fix this fence as soon as possible. It is a potential hazard to young children and should be fixed immediately.

Cordially,

Jane Alexander
Principal

Document Analysis

Here's a request for action that misses the mark. The writer describes a potentially dangerous situation and then asks (rather weakly) at the end of the letter for action.

Underline the purpose of the letter. Jot down an opening sentence that expresses this purpose.

Can you think of a way to strengthen the writer's efforts to get action on this request?

Has this principal covered all the bases? What legal problems could follow?

TEMPLATE C2-2. AFTER
PURPOSE: TO REQUEST ACTION
AUDIENCE: COMMUNITY MEMBER
TONE: AUTHORITATIVE
ORGANIZATIONAL STRATEGY: PROBLEM-SOLUTION

BUSINESS LETTER	Document Analysis
January 26, _____	
Mr. Pete Smith, President Cherokee Fencing Company PO Box 100 Detroit, MI 30032	
RE: Immediate Repairs to School Fence	Subject line.
Dear Mr. Smith:	
I will call you Friday morning to find out when you will be able to complete the repairs of the new fencing surrounding the primary children's recreational area. This problem was first noted by the teachers more than two weeks ago on January 12, and should have been fixed immediately to eliminate the potential danger for our students. As you know, this fencing protects the children from a very busy thoroughfare in the community.	Indicates problem. Writer notifies the reader that she wants to know repair schedule. States action requested to fix problem situation.
As we discussed on January 13 after the teachers reported the problem and again on January 20, the two support posts have been pulled out of the ground. Our children could gain access to a main street by pulling or pushing the wire fence over.	Documents the events in case of future legal action.
I have every expectation that you will attend to this matter quickly. I have appreciated doing business with you and have no complaints with the quality of your work. However, if action is not taken within five days, I will have to refer this matter to the school's legal department.	No griping. No ranting. States the facts and what action will follow if the situation is not corrected.
Sincerely,	More formal closing.
Jane Alexander Principal	Notifies central office of potentially dangerous situation and action taken.
cc: David Richards, Assistant Superintendent for School Operations	The principal covers her exposed rear flank.

Before

March 10, _____

Mr. and Mrs. Dennis Warren
215 Southhold Drive
Medford, NY 11763

Dear Parent:

As discussed by phone/conference your son/daughter, _____, will be suspended from the bus for _____ school days from _____ to _____. He/she may begin riding the bus on _____.

Your son/daughter was suspended from riding the bus for _____

_____

This is your child's _____ bus referral. Three or more bus referrals will result in denying bus transportation to your child for the rest the quarter/or year. It will then be necessary for you to provide transportation to school.

We hope this will not become necessary.

Sincerely,

Keith Johnson
Assistant Principal

Document Analysis

Giving bad news to parents is never easy. However, when dealing with large numbers of students, it becomes inevitable.

Principals frequently write follow-up letters to parents about student behavior. One of the common traps is to write immediately using a computerized form letter.

What bothers you about this one?

How would you assess the tone of this letter?

Form letters can be useful time savers. Let's rewrite this letter so the parents feel your interest and concern.

More important, by creating a more individualized follow-up letter, you show sensitivity to the parents' viewpoint: THEIR KID!

TEMPLATE C2-3. AFTER
PURPOSE: TO INFORM
AUDIENCE: PARENT
TONE: BUSINESSLIKE BUT SUPPORTIVE
STRATEGY: DEDUCTIVE

BUSINESS LETTER

Document Analysis

March 10, _____

Mr. and Mrs. Dennis Warren
215 Southhold Drive
Medford, NY 11763

Re: Bus Suspension Notice

Subject line.

Dear Mr. and Mrs. Warren:

Formal greeting using parents' name.

Based on our discussion <u>yesterday afternoon</u>, I regret to inform you that <u>Shawn</u> will be suspended from the bus for <u>three</u> school days from <u>March 11-13.</u> He may resume riding the bus again on <u>March 14th</u>.

Confirms parent notification of the incident. States dates of suspension.

I assigned the bus suspension because <u>he pushed another student out of his seat and punched him in the back. The bus driver had to stop the bus and separate the boys. Shawn said the other boy called him a name and this started the incident.</u>

States reason for action taken. Note the use of the active voice.

Gives a description of the incident.

This is the <u>second</u> bus referral for Shawn. He was sent to the office for<u> throwing pencils out of the bus window in November and suspended for one day.</u>

Summarizes the status of bus referrals and action taken.

I have spoken to <u>Shawn</u> about the seriousness of misconduct on the bus. We discussed the importance of not distracting the driver and what could happen if the driver's attention is taken from the road by students pushing and hitting one another. I asked <u>him</u> to write a plan for improving his bus conduct.

Shows interest in the student. Reminds student of expected behavior and shares concern for his safety.

Focuses on problem solving.

We know you share our concern for the safety of your child and the safety of all the students who ride the bus. Please review the student handbook with <u>Shawn</u> and help <u>him</u> in writing a plan that will benefit <u>him</u>. You will note in the handbook that a third bus referral could re-

Indicates future consequences.

Redirects parent to school policy and procedures.

sult in denying bus transportation for at least 10 days. We certainly want to avoid this from occurring.

We are all counting on <u>Shawn</u> to do <u>his</u> part in keeping the bus safe.

Sincerely,

Keith Johnson
Assistant Principal

Offers encouragement.

This follow-up letter does four things:
creates the paper trail documenting the events, reinforces what was said to both student and parent, focuses on problem solving, and shows interest and concern about student.

Reevaluate your letters, especially form letters, for making the parents feel like their child is ONE in a MILLION and not just another nameless face.

Scan your letters to parents of students who are consistently in trouble. Do they all sound the same? Put yourself in the reader's shoes. How do you feel?

Before

May 4, _____

Dr. Kathy Chandler
Principal
Parks High School
1090 Ocean Avenue
Princeton, NJ 10045

Dear Kathy:

While reading the Education Section of the <u>Princeton Journal</u>, my attention was caught by the article stating that you were elected president of the New Jersey Association of Educational Leaders.

This is a well-respected group which has had many prominent presidents. I have been happy to work with both past presidents, Glenn Myers and Rhonda Pennington. The organization has a long and prestigious record

Document Analysis

Letters of congratulations can go a long way in building and maintaining collaborative relationships among school-community members.

Who doesn't like a pat on the back and a word of praise from peers and bosses.?

The key to this type of letter is
♦ sincerity,
♦ brevity, and
♦ acknowledging the successful behavior of the recipient.

for both political and educational impact in the state, which I hope you will continue during your term of office.

I will be looking forward to great things under your leadership next year.

With best regards,

Paula Henderson
Principal

Underline the words and phrases that praise the reader and offer congratulations.

We would guess you haven't found many.

Jot down the points you think should be emphasized.

TEMPLATE C2-4. AFTER
PURPOSE: TO CONGRATULATE
AUDIENCE: PEER
TONE: FRIENDLY
STRATEGY: TOPIC

BUSINESS LETTER

Document Analysis

May 4, _____

Dr. Kathy Chandler
Principal
Parks High School
1090 Ocean Avenue
Princeton, NJ 10045

Dear Kathy,

Friendly greeting to peer.

I was delighted to read in the Princeton Journal that you have been elected president of the New Jersey Association of Educational Leaders.

Identifies behavior you are praising or complimenting.

What a coup for the Association to get you! However, they have always managed to attract top educational leaders and you certainly have shown your expertise in that arena. Being named a High School of Excellence is not an easy task.

Supports expression of praise or congratulations with personal details.

I am confident that you will surpass anything done by your distinguished predecessors.

Closes with warmth and sincerity.

Congratulations and best wishes.

Your envious colleague,

More informal sign-off.

Paula Henderson
Principal

Before

April 12, ____

Dr. Alan Michaels
School of Education
North State College
Seattle, WA 88770

Dear Alan:

Just wanted to respond to your request for feedback about Springville's participation in the Teacher Job Fair on Saturday, 9 April 1997. Overall, Judy Wilkes and I were very pleased with the general organization of the fair. However, we were quite disappointed with the physical layout of the fair itself. I don't think there should have been breakout rooms for school representatives. Most of these rooms were quite small and we couldn't get out to mix with the students. We were very impressed with the caliber of the students who attended the fair. We saw a good cross section of students-minority/non-minority, men and women, and regular education/special education. I spoke to a number of students concerning the Springville School System in reference to our instructional needs in regular, special education, and vocational education. When the students learned that our school system was not located in the state, their interest seemed to wane. I realize this was a teacher job fair, but how about adding a leadership component to your masters program. We have a growing need to identify leadership talent. Job fairs would be an excellent way to interview aspiring school leaders. However, we found the day to be productive and would be interested in participating in future job fairs held at the college.

Sincerely,

Joseph Day
Principal

Document Analysis

A colleague has asked you to give feedback on an event you attended.

As you read this letter, underline the places where the writer shifts to another topic.

How many topics did you uncover?

What sequence would you suggest to meet the needs of the reader?

What makes this letter difficult to read?

TEMPLATE C2-5. AFTER
PURPOSE: TO EVALUATE
AUDIENCE: COLLEAGUE
TONE: OBJECTIVE
STRATEGY: ANALYTICAL

BUSINESS LETTER

Document Analysis

April 12, _____

Dr. Alan Michaels
School of Education
North State College
Seattle, WA 88770

RE: Teacher Job Fair

Provides a subject line.

Dear Alan:

Uses first name since this is a colleague.

Overall, we found the day quite productive at your first Teacher Job Fair and we would be interested in participating in future programs. In response to your request for feedback, here are my thoughts about the recent job fair we attended.

States purpose of letter.

POSITIVE POINTS

Divides analysis into two major headings.

♦ <u>Organization</u>. Judy Wilkes, our personnel director, and I were quite impressed with the general organization and the handling of logistics. The general session was very informative and provided an opportunity for each school system to introduce itself. All communications regarding the job fair were timely and we were able to plan our presentations and interviews well in advance.

Gives the positive points first. Keeps to one topic within the heading.

♦ <u>Student Diversity</u>. You had a good cross section of students. I spoke to a number of minority and non-minority men and women regarding our needs in the following areas:

Uses bullets and underlining to highlight and keep information accessible to the reader.

    Elementary/Middle/Secondary Education
    Special Education
    English as a Second Language
    Vocational Education
    Performing Arts and Physical Education

POINTS TO PONDER:

♦ <u>Teaching Jobs Out of State</u>. When the students learned that Springville was located out of the state, their interest waned. Perhaps this information could be communicated to students earlier.

Presents the negative points tactfully.

Offers a suggestion.

♦ <u>Physical Layout</u>. We were a bit disappointed. Keeping school representatives in one large room would have been better than sending us to breakout rooms located in various parts of the building. We were cramped for space and in between interviews we couldn't mix with students.

♦ <u>No Educational Leadership Programs at North State</u>. We have an increasing need to fill entry level leadership positions. What can you do about adding on to your masters program in educational leadership?

Thanks for inviting us to your Teacher Job Fair. I hope these comments will be helpful.

Cordially,

Sign-off is more friendly in tone.

Joseph Day
Principal

Exercise C2-1
IT's YOUR TURN

Return to your in-basket and choose an item that requires a business letter to an individual outside the school. Follow these steps in preparing your letter.

♦ Complete an Action Planning Sheet; note your starting time in beginning this writing task.

♦ Map your ideas before you write. You can either make a list or a mindmap. The point is to put all your ideas down on paper. Let's try a mindmap.

Action Planning Sheet

Starting Time:_____

What is my purpose in writing this letter?

Who is my audience?

What is the attitude of this audience?
Positive/Neutral/Negative?

What information do they need?

What tone do I want to convey?

GETTING STARTED

- ◆ Draw a circle in the middle of a blank sheet of paper. Write your topic AND purpose in the circle.

- ◆ Now sketch a line out from the circle for each main idea that comes to you. At the end of each branch draw a circle and jot down each main idea. Try not to edit or evaluate what you write. The important thing is to get the points you want to communicate down in front of you. Look at each circle and add more lines and circles for related ideas. Keep going until you have jotted down everything you want to include in the letter.

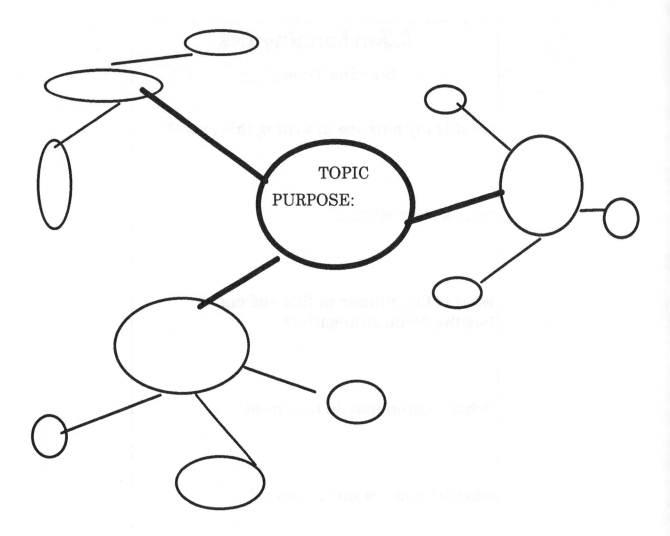

- Select an organizational strategy that will assist you in achieving your purpose. Refer to page 17 which outlines the ways you can structure the message. Which one will you use? If possible select a strategy that has been used in one of the "after formats" so you will have a visual example to model.

- Draft your letter. If you are using the disk, open file C2-6. Copy the template and write your letter.

TEMPLATE C2-6. YOUR BUSINESS LETTER
PURPOSE: _____
AUDIENCE: _____
TONE: _____
STRATEGY: _____

Document Guide

Somewhere Elementary

Kids Come First

10 Martin Lane
Anywhere, USA
23235

Design your letterhead to meet your purpose and attract the interest of the targeted audience.

Date Line _____

Inside Address _____

_____

_____

Reference Line

Dear _____:

_____

_____

_____

_____

Greeting

Begin Your Letter by:

♦ Getting the reader's attention.
♦ Telling the purpose.

_____

_____

_____

_____

_____

Develop your Letter by:

♦ Following your organizational strategy.
♦ Keeping paragraphs short (3-5 sentence on one topic).
♦ Using short sentences (18-20 words).

_____

_____

_____

_____

_____   **Conclude your letter by:**

_____   ♦ Emphasizing major
                                                              points.
_____   ♦ Declaring action
                                                              requested or needed.
_____
                                                          Select your closing.
_____
                                                          Sign legibly.
_____

_____

_____

Principal

_____   When appropriate include
                                                          the following:
_____
                                                          ♦ Reference Initials
_____
                                                          ♦ Enclosure Notation

                                                          ♦ Carbon Copy Notation

♦ Edit your letter for sentence clarity, word choice, grammar, punctuation, and spelling. Use your computer software tools to help check your writing.

♦ Create visually appealing letters by varying font size, highlighting, or underlining. Use graphics to support your purpose or relate to your audience. Design various letterheads that advertise the school's mission or latest achievement. Take the time now to experiment by replacing the graphics and school logo on this template to reflect your school.

♦ Make revisions and print the final copy. Note your completion time.

♦ Seek feedback from a trusted colleague.

SUMMARY

Letters and memos are written alternatives for our face-to-face communication. Like speaking, writing can convey information in a variety of nuances and formats. Whenever you think that you don't have the time to plan out your writing tasks, remember that confusing and poorly written letters waste the reader's time and can cost you loss of personal professional credibility and the credibility of your school. In summing up, Ellen Roddick (1986) provides six additional templates for you to consider in communicating your purpose.

When you want to:	Start your letter by:	Develop your memo/letter by:	Conclude your memo/letter by:
Inform	Introducing your topic.	Discussing or explaining it.	Summarizing the key points.
Persuade	Capturing your reader's attention with a novel slant or offer.	Bombarding your reader with convincing facts. Tell him or her what's the payoff.	Urging your reader to take action now.
Request	Telling what you want up front. Perhaps a gentle reminder on what you have done for the reader would help.	Offering good reasons for the request.	Showing appreciation for the help you are anticipating.
Complain	Announcing what's wrong.	Giving details about the problem.	Asserting clearly what you expect the reader to do to help remedy the situation.
Reject a request	Indicating sincere regret.	Clearly stating the decision for rejection and offering reasons why you cannot comply at this time.	Stressing the positive aspects or possible reconsideration at another time, if appropriate.
Congratulate	Expressing thanks or praise for a specific action.	Confirming your offer of good-will with personal or specific details.	Closing with genuineness.

Adapted from "Letters and Memos That Engage Readers." In *Writing That Means Business* by Ellen Roddick (1986). Macmillan, pp. 48-49.

References

Forbes, M. (1981). How to write a business letter. In *Business Communication*, Golen, S., Figgins, R., and Smeltzer, L. (Eds.) (1984). New York: John Wiley & Sons, pp. 78-81.

Joyce, A. (1991). *Written communications and the school administrator*. Boston, MA: Allyn and Bacon.

Minninger, J. (1992). *The perfect letter*. New York: Doubleday.

Roddick, E. (1986). *Writing that means business*. New York: Macmillan.

Watkins, F. (1982). Better business writing. In *Business Communication*, Golen, S., Figgins, R., and Smeltzer, L. (Eds.) (1984). New York: John Wiley & Sons, pp. 75-77.

Yerkes, D., and Morgan, S. (1991). *Strategies for success: An administrator's guide to writing*. Reston, VA: National Association of Secondary School Principals.

COMPETENCY THREE

REPORTS

COMPETENCY STATEMENT

Formulate penetrating reports that pave the way to understanding school-centered problems and accomplishments and projecting action plans to move the school forward.

KNOWLEDGE BASE HIGHLIGHTS

Watkins 1982. "The time and effort invested in producing a report only makes sense if the report passes this fundamental test. Is it useful to its audience? This will depend on the quality of the report's content and how well it is written."

Roddick 1986. The type of report you will have to write will affect how you organize your ideas. "The goal is to convey all the necessary information directly to readers without confusion or irrelevancies."

Joyce 1991. "As a school administrator, you are required to complete many reports and even more important you are personally liable for the accuracy of these reports. For example, accreditation may be withheld from a school if the self-study report is poorly done or if inaccurate information is reported."

STREAMLINING YOUR REPORTS

WHY ARE REPORTS TOUGH TO WRITE?

Compared with memos and letters, reports take time to develop. Watkins (1982) states that "they require more data, cover more territory in greater depth, and call for more detailed analysis." School administrators are responsible for reporting accurate information on all aspects of the school. You may be asked to submit a short or formal report on a wide range of topics. Keep in mind these critical elements:

WHAT ARE THE BASIC PARTS TO A REPORT?

Reports, whether they are short or long, break down into four basic parts:

SUMMARY

BACKGROUND

BODY

CONCLUSIONS/RECOMMENDATIONS

Writing each section of the report is like writing a paragraph. It requires a grasp of the key points and the ability to organize facts and information. The most important part of any report is the SUMMARY. Usually no longer than one page, the summary tells the reader what you're going to tell him or her. Generally, conclusions and reasons supporting them are the key elements of the summary. An effective approach in writing the summary is to use the 5 W's and H:

- **WHO** is reporting—district, school, department, team, individual?

- **WHAT** is the message and what is the evidence supporting the message?

- **WHEN** were the facts and findings gathered and **HOW** collected?

- **WHERE** did the information search take place?

- **WHY** is this report important and significant?

After reading the summary, the reader should know the key facts in each of these areas. Each section should cover the 5 W's and H in more detail. The body of the report is written first and then the summary. The bottom line in report writing is the same one for all types of writing—*Have you gotten the message across clearly and effectively?*

WHAT ARE THE COMPONENTS OF A FORMAL REPORT?

• Cover Letter	Prepares the reader by stating purpose and subject of report.
• Report Cover	Contains the title and date. Printed on heavy stock with attractive artwork if appropriate.
• Title Page	Identifies the subject and type of report. Ex: *A Proposal for an After-School Tutoring Program.*
• Table of Contents	Reports over four pages with several subsections need a table of contents to help the reader find information without searching through the report. Use the headings and subheadings of your report to develop the table.
• List of Figures and Tables	A list of graphs, charts, tables, and illustrations is placed before the report for easy access by the reader.
• Report Summary	Executive summary or abstract presents the essential information of your report in a concise way. Keep to one page.
• Report Text	The text of the report should include the following parts: *Introduction, Background, Body, and Conclusion.*
• Appendixes	Includes material that supports the purpose of the report but is not necessary. Ex: If you used a questionnaire in gathering data, you might want to include a copy of the survey.
• References	Materials used in preparing the report.

Five Report Writing Roadblocks

A roadblock is defined as an element from outside or inside oneself that causes temporary difficulty in reaching a goal. We know report writing can be a difficult task but knowing what to do and what to avoid may help you approach this task more quickly.

Roadblock #1: Ignoring Your Audience

Perhaps the gravest error for most administrators is ignoring or not thinking about the needs and attitude of the reader. Reports are usually directed to a specific person or group and has an explicit purpose. One suggestion is to ask the recipient of the report what information is needed and what can be eliminated. The point here is to make sure you have targeted the information required for the reader/committee to make a decision. It beats mindreading and having to go back and redo sections of the report.

Roadblock #2: Writing to Impress

Reports need to be understood on the first reading. Nothing turns off a reader faster than writing that is filled with educationese. Reports written with a highbrow impression may also hinder effective communication. Assuming your reader understands your vocabulary and your jargon is a serious *NO NO*. Your objective is this: *Make sure your reader comprehends your ideas with a minimum of misunderstanding.* Writing to impress is not limited to the use of ambiguous words but also includes nonessential detail and technical trivia. <u>Remember: short words, short sentences, short paragraphs!</u>

Roadblock #3: Dazzling with Data

A good painter not only knows what to put in a painting but, more importantly, he or she knows what to leave out. If you dazzle your readers with tons of information, they may be impressed but they may also miss the message. After each section of the report ask yourself these two questions:

♦ *"What can I remove from this paragraph or section without destroying its meaning and its relationship to what comes before and after?"*

♦ *"Does my reader require all this data to comprehend, evaluate, or make a decision with?"* (Vinci, p. 107)

By reducing excess words, descriptions, and supportive data, you will also reduce eye strain by your readers. In the end you will have a tighter, better, and more readable report.

ROADBLOCK #4: NOT ACCENTING

Failure to highlight the "significant elements, findings, illustrations, data, tests, facts, trends, procedures, or results" relative to your subject and purpose of your report will force your reader to do so. Consequently, he or she may consider the report incomplete, draw his or her own conclusions, or hit upon the recommendations by chance. "All the key points of your report should define and focus on the purpose of your report" (Vinci, p. 107).

Several methods may be used: <u>underlining an important statement or conclusion</u>, pointing out a particular illustration, using a different font size, **bolding a key recommendation**, utilizing headings and subheadings, and developing key sentences as the first or last sentence of a paragraph.

ROADBLOCK #5: OMITTING GRAPHICS

Here's where your technological expertise is going to pay off! The volume of data available to us as a result of technological advances "often makes it difficult to identify certain trends or patterns." As a school manager and decision maker "you are under a great deal of pressure and time constraints to read, evaluate and interpret data" (Golen & Ellzey, 1984, p. 109).

Did you know that a well-designed graph that fits on one page can summarize pages of written data? "Furthermore, when data are presented graphically, various trends and patterns can be recognized immediately" (Vinci, p. 109). Consequently, failure to utilize this tool may hinder your reader's decision-making time.

Your computer can design and generate tables, charts, graphs, drawings, and diagrams in COLOR. Use of these graphics can provide a powerful tool for management decision making and effective reports.

Adapted from Vinci, V. (1975). "Ten Report Writing Pitfalls: How to Avoid Them." In *Business Communications*, Golen, Figgins, and Smeltzer (1984). John Wiley & Sons, New York, pp. 102-108.

Adapted from Watkins, E. (1982). "Better Business Writing." In *Business Communications*, Golen, Figgins, and Smeltzer (1984). John Wiley & Sons, New York, pp. 99-101.

FRAMING A REPORT

Schools are communal agencies accountable to the public. Therefore, as a principal you are expected to gather information and present the status of all aspects of the school's operation. The audience and type of report you have to write will guide how you organize and present the data.

Resist the temptation to wait for the last minute to write a report. The results could be disastrous both to you and the recipient. Working against deadlines is a time management skill; working against deadlines when you dislike writing puts you at risk for major headaches. Breaking the writing project into manageable pieces and allocating time for each step is a way to attack the writing situation.

Here's a suggested way to begin.

♦ Use an action planning sheet which focuses you on your audience and purpose for writing.

♦ Generate your major ideas by listing them, outlining them, or drawing a mindmap.

♦ Relate your ideas by looking for major themes. When you have identified your major points, look for the details that support or relate to the main points that reinforce your purpose.

♦ Now select an organizational strategy to assemble your ideas in a meaningful pattern. Roddick (1986) tells us this: "People remember best ideas that are displayed in clear relationships... Readers aren't sponges, passively absorbing what they read. They read actively—judging, agreeing, disagreeing, interpreting, questioning. Write for an inquiring mind" (p. 53).

Roddick (1986) outlines several different ways to organize a report:

CHRONOLOGICAL

Your school experiences a break-in. You outline the sequence of events that led up to the break-in in the order of occurrence and present how the situation was handled. You give exact dates and time.

GEOGRAPHICAL

The school area has been redistricted. You discuss the effects of that on your school community area by area.

PROCEDURAL

Your school is implementing a new approach in scheduling students for academic classes. You explain the rationale for this change and the successive steps to be taken.

GENERAL TO SPECIFIC

You determine that the ninth grade failure is too high. You go from that generalization to the assessment of specific reasons that might be contributing to this generalization.

SPECIFIC TO GENERAL

You've come across a particular program that seems right for your school. You describe the program and develop a plan to show how this program might affect a certain grade or subject.

MOST TO LEAST IMPORTANT

You have additional funds in your school budget to purchase instructional resources. You assess the situation starting with the most crucial need and working down the list.

LEAST TO MOST IMPORTANT

You have been alerted to a rumor spreading in the community. You begin with the least alarming aspect of it and finally explain that something more serious did or did not occur.

CAUSE TO EFFECT

You have discovered a recurring problem in your computer system. You have to summarize the problems that have resulted from the school's use of that system in order to get it replaced.

EFFECT TO CAUSE

When observing one of your teachers you note the clear lack of classroom management skills. You must explain what has occurred and determine the possible causes for the performance.

PUT YOURSELF IN THE READER'S SHOES

Many states and professional organizations have encouraged local school systems to initiate innovative approaches to school improvement by providing grants. Here's an Innovation Report Proposal from a principal who seeks grant funds to support a local improvement effort in her school system.

Generally, most grant applications have specific criteria that the writer must address. The grant reader scores each proposal based on how the writer has addressed the critical elements outlined in the Request for Proposal (RFP) notification.

The successful grant writer meets the needs of the reader by nailing the criteria requested and making data presented accessible. Here's the criteria proposed in the RFP:

◆ School/Community Overview (10 pts)

◆ Evidence of Need (10 pts)

◆ Purpose, Objectives, and Activities to Meet the Need (20 pts)

◆ Evaluation Design (30 pts)

◆ Budget Breakdown (10 pts)

◆ Educational Significance (10 pts)

◆ Project Management (10 pts)

Exercise C3-1
GRANT REVIEWER

Read the following report and jot down in the margin where and how these elements are addressed. Each paragraph is numbered for easy reference.

Score the proposal.

Assess the written communication clarity of the proposal. What sections of the report did you have to read more than once? Mark them. Did you find this document difficult to understand? How so?

How would you score the writer for professional impact?

How many technical errors did you find?

Looking at the components of a report discussed earlier, what suggestions do you have for our colleague?

BEFORE

Increasing the Rate of School Completion by Students

Somewhere County School System
435 Harris Road
Haraldson, SC 34567

Riveredge Elementary
Susan Banks
Principal
PO Box 222
Haraldson, SC 34567

804/234-3434

Grant Request $4,900.

---

1. The problem of increasing the rate of school completion by students cannot wait until students are in high school, nor can the problem be sufficiently addressed at the middle school level. Children do not become at-risk students late in their public school program. Research has shown that the majority of at-risk students can be identified within the first three years of school. Therefore, to increase the rate of school completion for at-risk students, strategies must be implemented early in a child's education.

2. Those students who are at-risk, can in part be identified in their early school years by examining standardized test scores. For example, during the 1995-96 school year 43 students at Riveredge Elementary School had reading scores below the 25 percentile on the Criterion Reference Test. This number represents 56% of the students in the first grade. The percentage of

students in 1st grade who scored below the 35th percentile and qualified for Special Instructional Assistance (SIA) was 71. This high percentage of students scoring so low in reading on the CRT places them in the category of being at-risk.

3. Additional evidence for being at risk for so many 1st graders at Riveredge Elementary School comes from the reading subscores on the Iowa Test of Basic Skills (ITBS). The thirty-eight students who tool the reading section of the ITBS in March of 1990 scored either in the 1st or 2nd percentile. The average vocabulary percentile for this group of 1st graders was 23, and their word analysis skills average was in the 25th percentile.

4. For the 95-96 school year, 32% of the kindergarten students and 25% of the 1st grade students at Riveredge have qualified for the SIA program. Fifty-two percent of the 2nd graders currently enrolled at Riveredge Elementary are receiving remedial reading instruction either through Chapter I or the Remedial Education Program

5. In addition, 57 percent of the students qualify for the free or reduced lunch program. This is evidence of the low socioeconomic status from which many of the students come. With so many of the elementary students at Riveredge identified as being at-risk, it is apparent that many of these students will not stay in school long enough to complete a high school education. A program must be developed that will address the problem of reaching these at-risk students early in their educational program and encouraging them to stay in school.

6. Teale (1981), reports that research indicates that children who become early readers and who show a natural interest in books are likely to come from homes in which parents, siblings, or other individuals have read to them regularly. Frequent story reading at home help children become familiar with book language and recognize the function of written language. The fact that story reading are pleasurable and a social event builds a desire and interest in reading. Continual exposure to books develops children's vocabulary and sense of story structure, both of which help them learn to read.

7. A book release by Trelease (1989), gives the findings of a research study which indicate that children who were read aloud to on a regular basis showed statistically significant improvements in reading attitudes, independent reading, and comprehension skills. Trelease also estimates that only 20 percent of the parents and 30 percent of the teachers regularly read aloud to children.

8. Although reading aloud to children in practiced by some adults and teachers, the majority of children are not read to on a regular basis. The approach

to increasing the rate of school completion by students should begin in the early years of education. Young children should have books read aloud to them on a regular basis by parents and teachers. Research has shown that children who are read to develop larger vocabularies, have longer attention spans, and have the fewest difficulties in learning to read.

9. At Riveredge Elementary School a program will be developed to encourage parents to read aloud to their children on a regular basis. The focus of the program will be parents who have children in grades K-2. Teachers in grades K-2 will also be encouraged to read-aloud to their students each school day.

10. The specific components of the read aloud program can be divided into several major steps:

11. A series of inservice workshops will be held for the K-2 teachers about the positive effects of implementing a read-aloud program. The inservice program would also serve to help the teachers encourage the parents of their students to participate in the read-aloud program.

12. Parents of the students in grades K-2 would be contacted and encouraged to join the read-aloud program. Workshops would be held to teach the parents about the positive benefits of reading aloud to their children, and methods of reading aloud to them.

13. Teachers in grades K-2 would implement a read-aloud program daily in their classrooms.

14. The read-aloud efforts of the parents would be monitored. Parents would receive encouragement from school personnel, and they would receive books from the media center to read to their children.

15. Children involved in the read-aloud program would be given free books each month that they are in the program

16. The population of Somewhere School System is approximately 25,0000. However, the county remains a vast rural area with the population centered in three small cities.

17. Somewhere County has had a tremendous increase in population during the last fifteen years due to the installation of the Bay Naval Submarine Base. During this time the population of the county has more than doubled. However, the majority of the growth has centered in the southern part of the county where the cities of Haraldson and St. Andrew are located. The Bay Submarine Base is adjacent to the city of St. Andrew.

18. The naval submarine base has greatly affected the growth of Somewhere

County school system. Since the construction of the base, two elementary schools and two middle schools have been constructed.

19. Other schools already in service during this recent construction boom included three elementary schools and a high school. The cities of Lakeland, St. Andrews, and Haraldson each have an elementary school. The present high school is located in St. Andrew.

20. The target group for this program will be the students in grades K-2 at Riveredge Elementary School. The school has a population of 450 students in grades K-5 and 65 faculty and staff members. There are approximately 225 students in grades K-2. The ethnic balance of the students is almost equal. Forty-seven percent of the children are Black and Fifty-three percent are Caucasian.

21. The results of this approach cannot be measured directly, in a limited amount of time, to determine the overall effect of the program on increasing the rate of school completion by students. However, intermediate measurements can be taken. The percentage of the parents who participate in the program can be measured. It is anticipated that at least 50% of the parents of students in grades K-2 will participate in the read aloud program. Questionnaires can be given to the parents to determine the amount of time spent reading and the frequency of the reading they give their children. The number of books checked out to parents for the read-aloud program can be determined by examining media center records. Teachers' lesson plans can be examined for read-aloud segments.

22. Another method of evaluation is the results of tests scores of the students in the grades involved the program. It is anticipated that there will be a significant increase in the average test scores of the children who participate in the read-aloud program.

23. It is important to remember that the love of books by children is not easy to measure in educational terms. By offering a read-aloud program to students and having their parents involved too, it is anticipated that these children will develop a greater love of books which will increase their chances of staying in school.

24. This program could be adopted by other school systems at a very low cost. Workshops could be conducted by local personnel and books for the program could come from the media center or public libraries. School systems may have to alter the part of program of giving free books to students, but local service organization might be interested in providing free books. The read-aloud program can be adopted by any school or school system at a very low cost.

25. REFERENCES CITED

26. Teal, W. (1981). Parents reading to their children: What we know and need know. <u>Language Arts, 58</u>, 902-911.

27. Trelease, J. (1989). <u>The new read-aloud handbook</u>. New York: Penguin

Document Analysis

Here's how we evaluated this proposal.

First, the title of the proposal is misleading. The principal sees as a long-term goal the increase in the rate of school completion within the school system; however, the immediate objective is to increase student reading scores and attitudes toward reading in grades K-2. Therefore, we changed the title to:

Read-Aloud Intervention Program for Grades K-2
to Increase Reading Skills

Our well-intentioned colleague fell into Roadblock #1. By ignoring the needs of the reader, she has not targeted the information required for the reader to make a decision in her favor. She did not address the following sections at all:

- Budget Breakdown
- Project Management

The following sections were addressed but not clearly and not with enough information to make a favorable decision. These sections were weighted heavily and required more detail.

- Evaluation Design
- Purpose, Objectives, and Activities

By failing to use headings and subheadings to identify the important elements (Roadblock #4—Not Accenting), the writer forces the reader to do so. In this case, we conclude this proposal is incomplete and score it at the low end.

Furthermore, the writer has submitted a professional document that shows problems in the following areas. Here are some examples:

Writing Problem	Examples
Document Organization	No clear organizational tactic is evident. Paragraphs shifts in topic. Failure to use headings, subheadings and other highlighting techniques make the report hard to read.
Paragraph Organization	Paragraphs generally stick to one topic but consistently are limited to one or two sentences. Main ideas are not fully supported or explained.

Sentence Clarity	Sentences are generally clear and concise. The average sentence length is about 18-20 words. However, there are several sentences that display awkward structure.
Grammatical Errors	Paragraphs #6 and #7 show errors in verb-subject agreement. ...*reading* at home *help* ...the fact that story *reading* are pleasurable... ...research *study* which *indicate*
Punctuation	Paragraphs #4 and #15 reveal no periods at the end of sentences. Paragraph #20 incorrectly capitalizes the word *Fifty*
Spelling/Word Choice	Paragraph #3- *tool* for took Paragraph #8-*in* for is Paragraph #17-*tremedous* for tremendous Paragraph 20 -*Causasian* for Caucasian

How many others did you find?
Here's the rewrite.

TEMPLATE C3-1. AFTER
PURPOSE: TO PERSUADE
AUDIENCE: GRANT REVIEWER/FUNDING AGENCY
ORGANIZATIONAL STRATEGY: TOPIC/RFP CRITERIA
TONE: BUSINESSLIKE

**Read-Aloud Intervention Program for Grades K-2
to Increase Reading Skills**

SCHOOL COMMUNITY OVERVIEW

The population of Somewhere County is approximately 25,000. The county is primarily a vast rural area with the bulk of the population nestled in three small cities located near the coastline: Lakeland, St. Andrew, and Haraldson. Somewhere County has recently experienced a tremendous increase in population during the last fifteen years due to the installation of the Bay Naval Submarine Base, sprawling adjacent to the city of St. Andrew. During this time the population of the county has more than doubled, particularly in the southern part of the county.

The addition of the naval submarine base has greatly affected the growth of Somewhere County School System. Since the construction of the base in 1981 two elementary schools and two middle schools have been built. Other schools already in service during this construction boom include three elementary schools and a high school. The cities of Lakeland, St. Andrew, and Haraldson each have an elementary school; the present high school is situated in St.Andrew.

EVIDENCE OF NEED

High school dropout rates are particularly high in Somewhere County. Recent system-level data show that 40 percent of the entering freshmen do not complete their senior year. The problem of increasing the rate of high school completion cannot wait until our students reach these grades nor can the problem be sufficiently addressed at the middle school level. Children usually do not become at-risk students late in their educational program. Research shows that the majority of at-risk students can be identified within the first three years of school. Therefore, to ultimately impact on the high school dropout rate, strategies must be implemented early in our educational system to increase student achievement and interest in lifelong learning.

Riveredge Elementary School is a K-5 school with approximately 550 students. For the 1996-97 school year, 32% of the kindergarten students and 25% of the first grade students qualified for the Special Instructional Assistance (SIA) program in the county. Fifty-two percent of the second graders currently enrolled at Riveredge are also receiving remedial instruction either through Chapter I or the Remedial Education Program. It becomes clear that Riveredge is serving a student population that is at high risk for academic difficulty and possible high school failure. Results from standardized tests confirm this observation. For example, 38 students who took the reading portion of the Iowa Test of Basic Skills in March 1996 scored in either the first or second percentile. The average vocabulary percentile for this group of 1st graders was 23; their word analysis skills average was in the 25th percentile. Another example is the result of the county's Criterion Reference Tests. During the 1996-97 school year 43 students at Riveredge show reading scores below the 25th percentile on the CRT. This represents 56% of the students in the first grade.

PURPOSE, OBJECTIVES, AND ACTIVITIES

Teale (1981) reports that children who become early readers and who show a natural interest in books are likely to come from homes in which parents, siblings, or other individuals read to them regularly. Frequent story reading at home helps children to become more familiar with books and language and to recognize the function of written expression. Young children find story reading a pleasurable social event that cultivates a desire and an interest in reading. The research in this area also shows that exposure to books develops both vocabulary and a sense of story structure which helps children to learn how to read.

According to Trelease (1989), children who were read-aloud to on a regular basis showed statistically significant improvements in reading attitudes, independent reading frequency, and comprehension skills. Trelease also asserted that only 20 percent of parents and 30 percent of teachers read aloud to children on a regular basis. The researcher concluded that young children should have books read aloud to them on a regular basis since those children who are read to develop larger vocabularies, have longer attention spans, and experience fewer difficulties in learning how to read.

The purpose of this proposal is to establish a read-aloud program at Riveredge Elementary in grades K-2 in order to achieve the following objectives:

1. To improve students' attitudes toward recreational reading.

2. To improve students' attitudes toward academic reading.

3. To improve listening comprehension ability.

4. To improve reading ability.

The objectives would be achieved through the following activities:

Objective #1: To improve students' attitudes toward recreational reading.

Activity 1.1. Two general information meetings would be held for both K-2 teachers and parents about the positive effects of implementing a read-aloud program in grades K-2.

Activity 1.2. A series of four workshops would be scheduled for all K-2 teachers and parents interested in participating in the Read-Aloud Program. These workshops would be conducted by consultants from the local university who specialize in early childhood education. Teachers and parents would be trained in story telling methods and techniques for young children.

Activity 1.3. Parents would implement the read-aloud program at home.

Objective #2: To improve students' attitudes toward academic reading.

Activity 2.1. Teachers in grades K-2 will design and implement a read-aloud program daily in their classrooms.

Activity 2.2. Children involved in the read-aloud program will be given free books each month that they participate in the program in order to build a home library. These books would expand on the academic program whenever possible.

Objective #3. To improve listening comprehension ability.

Activity 3.1. Teachers in grades K-2 will question students about the main ideas in the read-aloud stories and ask students to tell these stories to parents at home.

Activity 3.2. Students will keep a log of best-liked stories.

Activity 3.3. Parents will also question their children about the read-aloud stories. Teachers will provide guided question and vocabulary sheets to parents.

Objective #4. To improve reading ability.

Activity 4.1. Teachers will develop teacher-made tests to monitor the comprehension and vocabulary skills of each student in the program.

EVALUATION DESIGN

Purpose, Population, Target Sample

The purpose of this program is to increase reading scores and attitudes of students in a rural elementary school. The school has a population of 550 students in grades K-5 with 65 faculty and staff members.. Fifty-seven percent of the students qualify for the free or reduced lunch program; 30 percent of the students are Hispanic, 20 percent are Afro-American, and 50 percent are Caucasian. The target group for this project will be students in grades K-2 at Riveredge Elementary School. There are approximately 225 students in grades K-2 who come from a blend of traditional and one-parent family settings.

Project Evaluation and Design

In any new approach to learning it is important to be able to assess the impact of the technique on student learning. The objectives stated earlier fall into two main categories: improved school climate regarding reading and improved reading scores on standardized tests. Since all the students in K-2 will be involved in the program, indirect comparisons will be made involving children enrolled in these grades prior to the onset of this project.

The following instruments will be used to collect data as they relate to the four objectives cited earlier.

Objectives	Evaluation Methods	Evaluation Instrument	Test Dates
1. To improve attitudes toward recreational reading	• Self-report attitude measure • Library check-out records • Student response journals • Parent and teacher observations and questionnaires	ERAS Recreational subscale	Fall 97 & Spring 98
2. To improve attitudes toward academic reading	• Self-report attitude measure • Student response journals	ERAS Recreational subscale	Fall 97 & Spring 98
3. To improve listening comprehension ability	• Standardized testing	SDRT Auditory Vocabulary subtest	Fall 97 & Spring 98
4. To improve reading ability	• Standardized testing	ITBS Comprehension and Vocabulary subtests	Fall 97 & Spring 98

Instruments

Iowa Test of Basic Skills (ITBS). This battery comprises numerous subtests, two of which assess instructional objectives addressed in both the experimental (Read-Aloud Program) and control settings (Students enrolled in K-2 classes before program was infused). These subtests are Reading Comprehension and Vocabulary. The ITBS is currently administered as a matter of county policy; the lowest level at which the instrument is given is second grade. Therefore, this test will provide an index of achievement at the end of the project's targeted group (K-2).

Elementary Reading Attitude Survey (ERAS). This self-report instrument measures two dimensions of children's attitude toward reading: academic (school-related) reading and recreational reading. The test is limited to children in grades 1-6 so the kindergarten students in this project will not be tested.

Stanford Diagnostic Reading Test (SDRT). This group-administered diagnostic instrument is a highly regarded screening tool for children experiencing reading difficulties. Its lowest level is designed for first and second graders and will be administered in the spring to children in both these grades. Of the entire battery, only the Auditory Vocabulary subtest will be given. This non-reading subtest assesses the extent of children's listening vocabulary through the use of sentence contexts so that the subtest is as much a measure of comprehension as vocabulary.

Data Collection and Analysis

All data will be collected by faculty and staff on site. The extent to which the project's objectives are accomplished will be determined by the following means:

Objectives 1-3. The first three objectives involve using test instruments not previously used at Riveredge. Therefore, a repeated measure comparison will provide evidence of change as students pass from first to second grade under the project. Students at both grade levels will be compared with their predecessors at these grades immediately prior to the onset of project activities. Library check-out histories, student journals, and parent/teacher observations and questionnaires will generate additional data that may help in describing how the effects have been brought about and the extent of the formative changes desired.

Objective 4. Improvement in global reading ability will be demonstrated by performance on the ITBS Reading Comprehension and Vocabulary subtests. These test are administered only in the spring of students' second-grade year so that they provide an overall indicator of the project's effectiveness at increasing reading skills. The control group will consist of students currently enrolled in second grade (96-97)

BUDGET

Total Funds Requested: $4,900.

♦ Orientation Sessions—	Local School Contribution
♦ Workshops (4 Days) Two consultants at $200 each per day— Travel—	$1600.00 Local School Contribution
♦ Books for Recreational and Academic Reading—	$2,000.00
♦ Reading Management Cards—	$300.00
♦ Test Materials—	$1000.00
TOTAL—	$4,900.00

PROJECT MANAGEMENT

The principal will serve as the project manager for this program with assistance from the testing coordinator at the system level. The principal will schedule the workshops and work closely with faculty and parents through each phase of the project. The test coordinator will take major responsibility for testing administration, data collection and project evaluation. The local system has agreed to support this effort for three years in order to assess the impact of the project on K-2 students during this time frame. The school's PTA has also agreed to support this program through fund-raising activities and parent support groups.

EDUCATIONAL SIGNIFICANCE

A positive attitude toward reading and learning is not easy to measure in educational terms. More important, a positive attitude toward school and life-long learning is even more difficult to sustain for many students as they proceed through their academic careers. However, we must start somewhere. By offering a read-aloud program to students in the K-2 grades it is anticipated that these children will develop a greater appreciation for books and learning, which we expect will increase their recreational and academic reading performance. Early success in reading and consistent support from parents and teachers should provide the foundation for better attitudes and performance during these early years. The long-term goal is to increase the system's high school completion rate, but steps to meeting this goal must start in kindergarten.

REFERENCES CITED

Teal, W. (1981). Parents reading to their children: What we know and need know. *Language Arts* (58), 902-911.

Trelease, J. (1989). *The new read-aloud handbook*. New York: Penguin.

Exercise C3-2
GRANT REVIEWER

As the grant reviewer, compare the "before" and "after" versions of this proposal. What made the second draft easier to read? What information was added and why? How did this additional information assist you as the decision maker?

Exercise C3-3
IT'S YOUR TURN

- ◆ Collect at least three reports you have recently written.

- ◆ Analyze these reports using the information discussed earlier in the following areas:

    Basic Components
    Report Writing Roadblocks
    Framing a Report

- ◆ Based on your analysis, what will you do differently the next time you write a report?

- ◆ Ask your immediate supervisor for a copy of a report that he or she thinks is well written.

- ◆ Compare your reports with this sample from a colleague.

REFERENCES

Golen S., and Ellzey, G. Communicating with graphics: A picture can be worth a thousand words. In *Business communication,* Golen, S., Figgins, R., and Smeltzer, L. (Eds.) (1984). New York: John Wiley & Sons, pp. 109-115.

Joyce, A. (1991). *Written communications and the school administrator.* Boston, MA: Allyn and Bacon.

Roddick, E. (1986). *Writing that means business.* New York: Macmillan.

Vinci, V. (1975). "Ten report writing pitfalls: How to avoid them." In *Business Communication,* Golen, S., Figgins, R., and Smeltzer, L. (Eds.) (1984). New York: John Wiley & Sons, pp. 102-108.

Watkins, F. (1982). "Better business writing." In *Business communication,* Golen, S., Figgins, R., and Smeltzer, L. (Eds.) (1984). New York: John Wiley & Sons, pp. 99-101.

COMPETENCY FOUR

SCHOOL FORMS, NOTES, AWARDS, AND BUMPER STICKERS

COMPETENCY STATEMENT

Design routine forms and public relation tools to reinforce outstanding performance and promote school successes.

KNOWLEDGE BASE HIGHLIGHTS

Tomlinson 1984. "As a professional educator, you are a professional communicator. You write and speak on many occasions. At times the amount of paperwork may seem quite overwhelming." Cut down on the paper load by seeking examples of best practice and modeling what your colleagues have already done well. Computer technology affords you a "gold mine" of tested, useable letters, memos, and other writing types that can be adapted to meet your needs. Imitation, the greatest form of flattery, is free to operate.

Joyce 1991. "Principals need assistance in the area of written communication now more than ever. Many states require that school leaders demonstrate competency in written communication." However, the fact is that most educational administration programs do not pay attention to the written communication skills required of a professional educator.

Pawlas 1995. Positive feelings develop from a sense of belonging or being recognized for contributing to school success. Principals who reinforce outstanding performance through internal communications build "involvement, accountability, and productivity."

Building Your Template Correspondence File

Developing a variety of school forms and boilerplate memos, letters, notes, and performance awards can help make writing for different audiences and purposes easier and faster. These writing forms can become templates on your computer for quick and easy access by your office staff, teachers, and yourself.

Look at your school calendar for ideas. The items listed below are suggestions for what can be created in your *School Form and Template File:* The secret to success is ensuring that these tools are clear, concise, accurate, and sensitive to the needs of the reader. Computer technology should be used to customize these forms as often as possible. Review these suggestions and add others from your routine correspondence file.

July/August/September

Student registration forms
Health requirements
School calendars
Staff and visitor sign-in sheets
Welcome back letters
Staff back-to-school checklists
Name tags
School letterhead and memo formats

October/November/December

Student discipline referral forms
Student suspension letters/forms
Parent-teacher conference response forms
Volunteer programs
Teacher evaluations
Report cards
Field trips
Enrollment changes

January/February/March

Staff and student recognition notes/awards
Bumper stickers
Media release forms
Student progress

Checklists
Invitations

April/May/June

Response forms to field day activities
End-of-school checkout lists
Graduation
Certificates of award
Evaluation forms

STARTING YOUR TEMPLATE FILE

Here are several forms we have compiled to help you get started on those writing tasks that surface every year. Check with your colleagues on the forms and letters they use; get copies and add them to your file. You will soon have a sweeping resource of sample letters and forms to choose from in meeting your purpose, audience, and tone.

JULY/AUGUST/SEPTEMBER

TEMPLATE C4-1. WELCOME LETTER
PURPOSE: TO BUILD RELATIONSHIPS AND TO INFORM
TONE: FRIENDLY

Document Analysis

Dear Mr. and Mrs. Bass:

Welcome to _____!

Your daughter/son, _____, may have already chatted with you about the life here at _____ School—whether the other kids are friendly, what the teachers are like, the quality of the school lunches, and whether our school is easier or harder than the school he/she last attended. We like to think that after the first ten days all new students feel accepted and comfortable in our learning community.

We are pleased to have you as partners in our educational family. As the year progresses, and you become either more informed or more puzzled, we encourage you to call the school and talk with those who might be of

The writer wants to greet new parents in an amiable and courteous manner.

The letter is customized to reflect the student's name.

help. If your question deals with in-class events, please ask to speak with the teacher. If it deals with the overall program, curriculum, or activities, please contact me directly. The school has 24-hour voice mail assistance so you can leave us a message to contact you at any time convenient to your schedule. We also provide a Homework Hotline so you can find out what your child needs to do when illness or personal reasons prevent _____ from attending school.

One of our goals is to see that the parents and guardians of students—like the students themselves—feel at home at _____School. To accomplish this, Parent Newsletters are mailed to all students' homes throughout the school year, providing you with information about events and activities.

You will also want to look at _____'s copy of the student handbook. It does a good job of explaining a typical year at our school. By reading it, you will also have a better idea of what to expect.

We are glad to have you with us this year, and we want to assure you that we will do our best to help your child experience academic, social, and emotional success. With your help and support, this should be a very rewarding school year.

Cordially,

Rose Taylor
Principal

The writer provides the new parents with useful information:
♦ 24-Hour voice mail
♦ Homework hotline
♦ School Newsletter
♦ Student Handbook

Invites parent support.

Sign-off matches the tone of the letter.

Template C4-2. Back-to-School Memo to Staff
Purpose: To Motivate; Build Relationships
Tone: Collaborative

TO: All Faculty and Staff Members
FROM: Your Fearless Leader
SUBJECT: Return to School

A new school year presents opportunities for new beginnings—new classes, new faces, sometimes new teaching assignments, and often new ways of conducting business. Summer vacation can be a great rejuvenator; and

Document Analysis

What do you say to returning staff besides?

"Welcome back. Now get to work!"

This principal wanted to inspire and motivate his staff.

as we approach the opening day of a new school year, the end-of-year problems and pressures that irked us in June seem remote and not so overwhelming.

Starting the new year gives us the chance to make new plans, design new teaming strategies, and implement new ideas. There is always room for self-improvement whether one's responsibilities are administering, supervising, teaching, preparing lunches, maintaining a building, or managing an office. The important thing is to plan for success.

We can be proud of what we do here at _____— in our classrooms, in our offices, and in our school community—but our achievements are not due to complacency and satisfaction with the status quo. Our program is what it is because you are dedicated to doing what is best for all students and are always searching for ways to achieve that goal.

This year, as in the past, we must focus on the processes that spur continual advancement: evaluating what we have, determining what we can do to improve, and identifying what we need to make those improvements happen. I look forward to working with each one of you and recognize the professional talent and commitment it takes to do a challenging job well.

Let's make 19__our best year yet!

TEMPLATE C4-3. STUDENT PROGRESS REPORT FORM
PURPOSE: TO INFORM
TONE: COLLABORATIVE
STRATEGY: NEED/PLAN/BENEFIT

Date: _____   **Document Analysis**

Student Progress Report
for

_____
(student's name)

Parent Signature and Comments: _____

_____

_____

_____

Dear Mr. and Mrs. _____:

We want to make sure that each of our students achieves academic and social growth here at _____ School. To attain this goal, our teachers prepare a written report early in the school year to provide you with useful information about _____'s adjustment and progress.

States need.

Identifies plan.

With your encouragement and support, we hope that your son or daughter will achieve the kind of progress you consider acceptable or commendable. If you are not satisfied with the performance shown on this report, there is still time for needed improvement prior to the end of the first report card period which ends on

_____.

Here's an effort to prevent problems from getting worse.

Academic Performance Areas

Math Teacher _____ Grade _____
Comments: _____
_____
_____

Parents want to be kept informed of their child's progress; the earlier the better.

Science Teacher _____ Grade _____
Comments: _____
_____
_____

Computers can make this happen. Forms like these can be put on disk, updated, and filed.

English Teacher _____ Grade _____
Comments: _____
_____
_____

Social Studies Teacher _____ Grade _____
Comments: _____
_____
_____

Electives/Exploratory Areas

PE Teacher _____ Grade _____

Comments _____

_____

_____

Art/Music/Band Teacher_____ Grade _____
Comments: _____

_____

_____

Our goal it to help each student meet success. We hope that by keeping you advised early in each reporting period, we can work together to meet this goal. Feel free to contact individual teachers (864-5657) or the guidance counselors (456-7894) if you have questions, concerns, or want to set up a parent conference. Please sign this report and have your son or daughter return it to the homeroom teacher.

Thank you,

Summarizes with benefits to all stakeholders.

Provides a contact number.

OCTOBER/NOVEMBER/DECEMBER

TEMPLATE C4-4. SCHOOL SUSPENSION FORM

Dear Mr. and Mrs _____:

Document Analysis

We regret to tell you that your son/daughter _____, has been suspended from school for _____ days. The suspension begins on _____ and ends on _____.

Gives purpose of the letter.

When a situation develops that interferes with the safety or learning of other students here at school, it then becomes necessary for the school to take action to correct it.

Provides rationale for action taken.

The reason for this suspension is as follows: _____

_____

_____

_____

The necessary information is supplied.

I have talked with _____ about this incident and he/she has agreed to write a plan on how to handle

Shows concern for student. Focuses on problem solving.

this situation should it arise again in the future. Please review this plan with your child and discuss your expectations about his/her behavior in this matter.

Shows appreciation for parent help.

You may also find it helpful to review the student handbook with your child. We know _____ will do his/her part in helping our school be the best it can be.

Thank you for your support,

Letters like these are never easy. The writer gives the information in a succinct, business-like way.

Template C4-5. Instructional Performance Appraisal Narrative Report

---

I. GENERAL INFORMATION

Document Analysis

Teacher _____ Topic _____ Grade _____

Subject _____ Period _____ Date _____

Teacher observation and evaluation can be difficult and time-consuming.

The following appraisal conforms to the district's guidelines for teacher evaluation. Criteria and descriptors are presented in those guidelines and pertain to three major performance areas:

The form you use—memos, checklists, self-evaluation questions, and post-observation reports—depends on your purpose and the status of the teacher.

♦ Productive Teaching Techniques

♦ Organized, Structured Class Management

♦ Positive Interpersonal Relations

♦ Probationary
♦ Tenured

Teaching Episode Summary

There are two keys to effective teacher evaluation:

<u>Beginning of Lesson</u>

While waiting for the bell, Mrs. Harris returned assignments, corrected tests, and collected field trip money. After completing these tasks, she indicated that today's lesson would involve finishing the background information for the Congress of Vienna (1815). The objectives of the lesson were written on the board: "To analyze the Balance of Power the Congress of Vienna sought to establish after Napoleon and to establish the alliances which would be necessary to maintain it."

♦ Being objective by using descriptive rather than judgmental language.
♦ Supporting your observations, conclusions, and recommendations with precise and specific detail related to the performance criteria.

Middle of Lesson

Through the use of board notes and questioning, Mrs. Harris progressed through the purposes of the international leaders of this time; the fate of France; and the terms established by the Congress of Vienna. Discussion took place concerning the role of France and European sentiments being anti-France or anti-Napoleon.

End of Lesson

The lesson concluded with a focus on Metternich and his role at this conference and in this time period. Questions were raised as to why Metternich dominated the Congress of Vienna. Mrs. Harris called on students to summarize the major points of the lesson. She gave a follow-up homework assignment and dismissed the class.

II. PERFORMANCE COMPETENCIES

Productive Teaching Techniques

1.1 Mrs. Harris is highly organized in her planning and preparation. Her lesson plans were detailed and she provided students with visual organizers to help with their notetaking skills. She also supplemented these outlines with extensive board notes and overhead transparencies.

1.2 Mrs. Harris' questioning technique has improved to reflect higher order thinking skills. Student responses were more analytical and reflective. Students supplemented the responses of peers and spontaneously questioned the position of one another.

1.3 There was some level of confusion on the part of students in two parts of the lesson. This could have been eased by prefacing the lesson with clear definition of terms such as *reactionary, conservative, liberal*, etc. The other need was the use of a set of European maps. Much that the students could not visualize might have been clarified by showing such maps.

Organized, Structured Class Management

2.1 Mrs. Harris minimizes the amount of classroom

The data are accessible and easy to find. The writer uses headings and sub-headings to organize the information.

The writer supports observations and conclusions with facts from the teaching episode.

time devoted to non-instructional activities. Attendance, distribution, and announcements were quickly and efficiently dispatched.

Interpersonal Relations

3.1 The atmosphere in the classroom has significantly improved. Mrs. Harris supported student responses by rephrasing and building on their comments and encouraging student questions and interactions. She has eliminated the use of sarcasm in her verbal exchanges.

III. PERFORMANCE SUMMARY

Mrs. Harris demonstrated above average skill in the three performance areas cited above. She has significantly improved in areas one and three.

Appraiser _____ Title _____

Signature _____ Date _____

Teacher's Signature _____ Date _____

JANUARY/FEBRUARY/MARCH

TEMPLATE C4-6. TEACHER OBSERVATION CHECKLIST

Directions: Circle the teaching indicators demonstrated during the lesson. In the comment section describe the quality of the performance.	Document Analysis
BEGINNING THE LESSON 1. Gains attention through a motivating, interesting, and/or stimulating introduction. 2. Focuses students' attention on the lesson objective or content to be learned. 3. Activates prior learning by reviewing previous lesson or links learning to students' life experiences.	Observing teachers is a time consuming task. Here's a checklist that outlines the effective teaching behaviors that could be occurring in any

4. Establishes the purpose of the lesson. **Comments:**	lesson.
<div style="text-align:center">**CONDUCTING THE LESSON**</div> **Lesson Input** 1. Develops content through a variety of instructional strategies such as lecture, discussion, cooperative learning, and small group work. 2. Provides meaningful associations to aid learning through the use of simile, metaphor, definitions, examples, illustrations, or demonstrations. 3. Presents the content in clear, easy to follow steps. 4. Sequences the content logically: easy to hard, simple to complex. 5. Breaks the learning into manageable segments; gives a model to follow and allows practice before moving to next step or concept. 6. Stresses the major, important features of the topic. 7. Uses auditory and/or visual aids to emphasize the main points. <div style="text-align:center">**Comments:**</div> **Student Involvement** 1. Allows students to work independently and apply what is being learned. 2. Provides a balance between delivery mode (teacher centered) and access mode (student centered). 3. Encourages student questions and comments. 4. Provides opportunities for students to practice and/or process the content. 5. Maintains student attention through appropriate pacing of instruction to keep students interested and on task. <div style="text-align:center">**Comments:**</div>	

<u>Checking for Understanding</u>

1. Asks clear content related questions.
2. Solicits a variety of responses from both volunteers and non-volunteers.
3. Modifies instruction based on the quality of students' understanding.
4. Provides feedback and reinforcement to students' work and responses.
5. Identifies students who are having difficulty and takes corrective action.

Comments:

ENDING THE LESSON

1. Provides closure through review, restatement of key points, follow-up activities, or other ways that summarize the lesson.
2. Provides enough time for students to have closure.
3. Maintains lesson activities until the end of the period.

Comments:

CLASSROOM MANAGEMENT

1. Distributes materials efficiently.
2. Avoids unnecessary delays, interruptions, and digressions.
3. Arranges teaching materials in an efficient way.
4. Monitors the students frequently and demonstrates withitness.
5. Provides clear directions and procedures.
6. Promotes on-task behavior.
7. Communicates expectations about behavior.
8. Provides appropriate non-verbal and verbal feedback about behavior when necessary.

9. Intervenes appropriately when behaviors disrupt learning or student is off task within one minute of initial occurrence. 10. Uses low level intervention strategies that do not disrupt the learning of the entire class. 11. Monitors the attention of students who have been redirected. <center>**Comments:**</center>	
<center>**RECOMMENDATIONS**</center>	

TEMPLATE C4-7. PARENT CONFERENCE FORM

Student's Name: _____ **Grade:** _____

Teacher: _____

Conference Date: _____ **Time:** _____

Conference Agenda

We are interested in your appraisal of your child's growth and development. During our conference time we would like to discuss _____'s progress in several areas. The following agenda is a suggested outline. Please feel free to jot down any questions or topics you would like to discuss. We look forward to seeing you.

Social/Emotional Characteristics

♦ Peer interaction

♦ Teacher interaction

Document Analysis

Often we set the agenda for many parent conferences.

Here's a conference form that invites parents to participate in the process.

Learning Strengths

- ◆ Completes work
- ◆ Organizes
- ◆ Thinks creatively
- ◆ Works independently

Academic Achievement

- ◆ Content strength areas
- ◆ Content growth areas

Problem-Solving Skills

- ◆ Able to make decisions
- ◆ Shows respect for people and ideas
- ◆ Persistent
- ◆ Able to generate solutions

Conference Questions/Concerns

_____
_____
_____
_____

Conference Outcomes

_____
_____
_____
_____
_____

TEMPLATE C4-8. LETTER OF RECOMMENDATION

Date line

Inside Address

RE: Letter of recommendation for _____

Dear _____:

Mr./Ms./Dr. _____ has asked me to write a letter of recommendation in support of his/her application for principal in the _____ County School District. I am happy to do so.

Through our association in the _____ Public Schools, Mr./Ms./Dr._____ and I have been acquainted for more than _____ years. He/she is earnest, resourceful, dynamic, and honest. He/she is a true leader.

For the past _____ years Mr./Ms./Dr. _____ has served in a demanding district as the assistant principal for _____School, responsible for instructional supervision, student discipline, and building maintenance. He/she has experienced many successes. He/she has chaired a complex scheduling and homeroom guidance program, evaluated teachers and staff, participated in personnel decisions, and written a detailed student code of conduct. In both daily routine and special assignments, I have observed his/her leadership skills, sense of humor, and tactful administrative style.

Mr./Ms./Dr._____communicates clearly and effectively in both oral and written expression. As a writer his/her communication is clear and concise. He/she initiated the staff newsletter in our school district. As a speaker, he/she demonstrates impressive presentation skills with faculty groups, students, and parents.

Mr./Ms./Dr. _____is a highly visible and

Document Analysis

Personnel directors receive hundreds of letters. By meeting their needs you will also help the person you are recommending.

Use a reference line to state your purpose.

Mention name of person and the position.

Mention your relationship and length of association.

Summarize professional experience.

Emphasize skills important to the job. Provide examples of those skills.

Stress results and achievements.

End with strong recommendation.

caring staff member. While working with him/her, I have been continually impressed with his/her driving commitment to excellence. He/she is relentless in his/her quest for school success for all students.

In my professional judgment, Mr./Ms./Dr._____ is a very effective school administrator. He/she has a high degree of skill in problem solving, organizational ability, and strategic planning. He/she has the interpersonal skills and the talent to perform very successfully as a principal.

If I can be of further assistance, please feel free to contact me.

Sincerely,

Make your task easier. When writing letters of recommendation ask the person to give you this information:
♦ Current resume
♦ Job announcement
♦ Name/address of person receiving the letter

Focus your letter on the responsibilities and skills outlined in the job description.

April/May/June

Template C4-9. Handclapping Notes

APPLAUSE NOTE

Document Analysis

Use your computer software to develop special ways to give someone a pat on the back.

TEMPLATE C4-10. SPECIAL RECOGNITION AWARDS

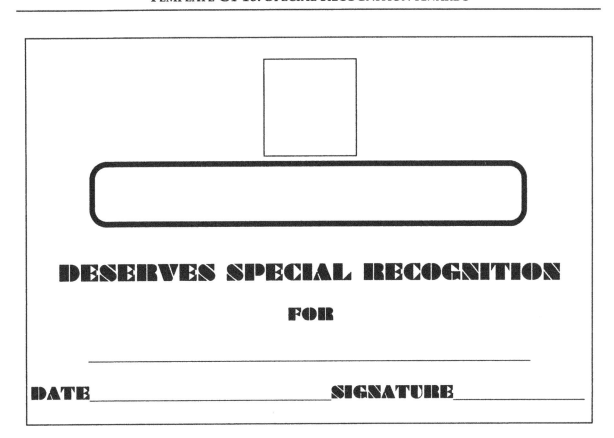

DESERVES SPECIAL RECOGNITION

FOR

_____

DATE_____**SIGNATURE**_____

TEMPLATE C4-11. SCHOOL BUMPER STICKERS

MY CH/LD EARNED THE **PRINCIPAL'S**

AWARD AT

MEDLOCK PARK MIDDLE SCHOOL
AUSTIN, TEXAS

Exercise C4-1
It's Your Turn

Create a medley of notes, awards, and bumper stickers to share the nifty things going on in your school. Remember, it pays to advertise. If you don't brag about your staff, students, and programs, who else will?

Summary

Pawlas (1995) tells us that sharing good news about staff, students, and the school is a communication "challenge a principal must accept." Not only is it important to recognize the efforts of those within the school community, it is becoming even more important to make sure members outside the school community stay in touch with and involved in the programs of the school. By developing a broad base of communication tools, principals can alert parents to the school's achievements and keep tax-paying citizens informed enough to make positive decisions toward the school at the voting box.

References

Joyce, A. (1991). *Written communications and the school administrator.* Boston, MA: Allyn and Bacon.

Pawlas, G. (1995). *The administrator's guide to school-community relations.* Princeton, NJ: Eye On Education.

Tomlinson, G. (1984). *School administrator's complete letter book.* Englewood Cliffs, NJ: Prentice Hall.

COMPETENCY FIVE

NEWS ARTICLES, PRESS RELEASES, AND TOP-NOTCH NEWSLETTERS

COMPETENCY STATEMENT

Publicize good news, student and staff achievement, and program results to build community support through effective public relations tools.

KNOWLEDGE BASE HIGHLIGHTS

Pawlas & Meyers 1989. The principal plays a key role in controlling both the quantity and quality of school communications. School leaders need to know how to develop both one-way (newsletters, bulletins, and media announcements) and two-way (surveys, questionnaires, and polls) communication types.

Joyce 1991. "A widely distributed newsletter or annual report can help present a positive image of the school. By writing news releases, newsletters, and annual reports, you can let your community know about the positive events happening in your school."

Vann 1992. Principals can forge an effective home-school partnership through monthly newsletters, writing a column in a parent organization newsletter, issuing parent and student handbooks, and other regular home-school publications.

Pawlas 1995. "When done properly, a school newsletter is a valuable public relations tool that generates not only interest but goodwill too. Studies have shown that parents rate the school newsletter as their second most important source of information about the schools."

WHY YOUR NEWS IS SPECIAL

The *New York Times*, according to Nancy Brigham with the UAW Local Union Press Association, says it carries "all the news fit to print." But who really decides what is "fit to print?" Unlike the mass media who depends on "stories to attract the readers advertisers want" (Brigham, 1991, p. 14), we have a real choice in deciding what information to communicate to our parents, students, and general community.

Community newsletters and stories fill the giant void left by mass media because they provide "news about people they know, neighborhoods they live in, places they work, and their own organizations." So if you're still asking yourself the question, "Why should I write news articles, press releases, and even produce a newsletter for my school?" remember you are part of the "alternative media." Brigham (1991) reports that "no matter how inexperienced you are as a newsletter producer, you are filling a vacuum by telling stories that are relevant to average citizens within their neighborhoods"; the stories that mass media won't print because they're not backed by big advertising bucks.

WHERE YOU FIT IN

How many times have you tried to get even your local paper to print a news story or article about your school? Well, if you're ready to beat the system here's where you can fill in the gaps. How about creating your own school newspaper or newsletter? The gap that only you can fill includes the following:

- Report news and information that goes beyond your school doors. Include interesting and helpful educational ideas for parents, students, and teachers.

- Offer well-rounded coverage of the events. Go beyond the 5 W's. The heroes of your newsletter or school paper are your students, teachers, parents, and peers, people who don't normally make the *Six O'clock News* but who deserve recognition.

- Don't be afraid to tell things as they are. Show how everyone is involved in the school's problems and successes. Help your school community to understand how the school operates with down-to-earth stories and explanations.

The Nuts and Bolts of News Writing

Communicating to your various school audiences requires a conversational type of writing. Who cares if you have a Ph.D.? If you make your parents feel dumb because they can't understand the message, what have you gained? What's more important, what have you lost?

Writing articles for your school newsletter requires a different approach. Unlike the organization of letters and memos (introduction, body, conclusion), articles for newsletters follow the format used by newspapers—the inverted pyramid. Follow these steps in writing articles and news releases:

Answer the 5 W's and H: Who, What, When, Where, Why, and How

The first paragraph should capture the attention of the reader. Paint word pictures to keep your readers interested. Use words that are familiar but help your readers to see, hear, feel, smell, or touch as they read along. Read the following examples. Which grabs your interest? Why?

Example: Mabry High School has been notified by the University of Georgia in Athens that Mark Anderson, son of John and Karen Anderson, has been awarded two scholarships. The first is a scholastic honor scholarship based on academic achievement, and the second is a music scholarship.

Example: Mark Anderson, a Mabry High School Senior, seized two college scholarships from the University of Georgia in Athens. For high academic achievement he snared a scholastic honor scholarship and for his artistic abilities he nabbed a music scholarship.

Develop Following Paragraphs by Expanding on the Details Announced in the First Paragraph

Each paragraph should focus on one topic. Start with what interests your readers and then give them the facts or supporting evidence. Keep your sentences short by using small words. For example:

help for assistance
fair for equitable
<u>choose</u> for designate
action for implementation

Limit the paragraphs to two or three sentences.

Present the Most Important Information First. Arrange Facts in Order of Descending Importance

Sequence your paragraphs with the key information presented first. Then follow up with the details you think will interest your reader most. Often newspapers need to cut the length of news articles to make room for cutting edge stories or events.

Use Direct Quotes and Pictures to Keep the Reader's Interest

End with a bang. Leave your reader with a new idea, possible solution, or an insightful quote. Remember: a picture is worth a thousand words.

Write a Snappy Headline

1. Answer the reader's question, "Why should I bother reading this?"

2. Keep the caption between three to eight words.

3. Use the present tense.

4. Stick to short familiar words.

5. Set the headline in **BIG, BOLD TYPE.**

6. Edit your headline for unnecessary words.

7. Consider using a question as a headline.

Here are two news articles that reflect the suggestions listed above. What do you think?

Template C5-1. News Article

	Document Analysis
Carolyn Johnstone, an English teacher at Milton High School, has written a book about adolescents with attention deficit disorders. Recently published by Teachers Press Inc., it is entitled *High Schoolers with Attention Deficit Problems: A Survival Guide*.	The first paragraph states the key information. Answers the 5 W's.

A prepublication reviewer in Publishers Network wrote that the book "shows parents and students practical ways to cope with the demands of the high school curriculum particularly as it impacts on students' ability to organize information and produce written products. Ms. Johnstone provides useful and results oriented strategies for parents and students to try as they search for ways to make high school a successful experience."

Starts the second paragraph with an idea to grab interest—student success in high school.

Each paragraph focuses on one idea.

The author, a native of New York, has taught English at Milton High School for the past five years. Prior to that, she taught English for four years at Dodgen High School located in Atlanta, Georgia. Ms. Johnstone has written numerous articles for professional journals on the teaching of English.

Gives details about the author.

The paragraphs are presented in descending order of importance.

The book concerning attention deficit disorder in adolescents "took longer than I expected," Ms. Johnstone noted. "Attention deficit disorder is a serious problem for many teenagers, especially boys. Many of these students are bright, capable and want to learn. If we, as parents and teachers, cannot find ways to help them be successful, I'm afraid they will lose hope and drop out of school. We must try."

The article could be cut after any one of the paragraphs.

Ends with a quote.

TEMPLATE C5-2. NEWS ARTICLE

Document Analysis

Sharon Hodges was named Tipton County's *Middle School Teacher of the Year* for 1997. Ms. Hodges did not intend to be a teacher. A history major in college, she wanted to be a librarian. She only pursued her teaching credentials because she had several additional courses to take. However, after her student teaching experience, she knew the classroom was the only place for her. "Once I got in the classroom, I loved it. I feel bad now when someone tells me they don't love their job."

Answers the 5 W's in the first paragraph.

Uses a quote from the teacher.

Ms. Hodges explains she always gets a sense of helping others when one of her students masters a skill or has

Paragraphs are sequenced in descending order of

matured in her classroom. She wants every student in her class to think, "This teacher really cares about me and wants me to be successful."

To accomplish this goal, Sharon Hodges tries to make her social studies classes as exciting as possible, and teaches things which are interesting and stimulating to her as an adult learner. She also tries to make social studies come alive for her eighth grade students.

To help her students retain and apply the information learned in class, she is a firm believer in both individual and group learning approaches. "Real learning happens when the students are doing the work. I try to involve all the senses in helping students to master concepts and learn new skills," she said.

Ms. Hodges calls her students' parents on a regular basis. They "are paying the bills and I want them to know how well their child is doing." She feels it is important to establish a positive relationship with parents and to seek their support and involvement in her interaction with students.

She is also very active with student organizations and attends many activities that her students may be involved with. She believes that "more connections" make better communications between her and her students. Ms. Hodges believes that while doctors save bodies and preachers save souls, teachers save dreams and futures.

importance.

Each paragraph expands on the key information presented in the first paragraph.

Paragraphs are short.

Uses lots of quotes to keep interest.

Ends with an insightful thought.

Exercise C5-1
Writing a Headline

Both the preceding news articles need attention-getting headlines. Using the suggestions described earlier, create a headline for each of these news stories.

Press Releases

As the principal reporter in your school, it's your job to decide what your parents and general community members need to know about your staff, students, and program accomplishments. Pawlas (1995) tells us that local newspaper reporters look for news stories that fit into one of these categories.

- ◆ Unusual twist or slant
- ◆ Timely
- ◆ Appealing to the average citizen
- ◆ From a famous or expert source
- ◆ Human interest
- ◆ A demonstration of results

News releases need to be developed regularly to get out the school's story to the general public in a timely way. Pawlas (1995, p. 116) suggests "to expedite the process and ensure that the necessary details are contained in the news release, a standardized format should be used" to collect the needed data. Here's a sample of a news-gathering format used in one school system.

TEMPLATE C5-3. SCHOOL NEWS NOTES

Lexington County School District Five

NEWS NOTES

Please Print

Teacher_____School _____
Grade _____Unit Name/Subject _____

Activity_____
Time_____Date _____Place_____

Purpose of the
Activity_____
_____
_____
_____

Number of People
Involved_____

Special Dress or Props_____

Teacher's Planning Period_____Contact Number _____

**Return to: Lynn Long, News Coordinator, Leaphart Elementary
School**

Exhibit 6.5 News Note taken from Pawlas (1995), *The Administrator's Guide to School-Community Relations*. Eye On Education. Reprinted with permission, p. 117.

Exercise C5-2
SCHOOL NEWS NOTES

Design a news-gathering format that will help you collect interesting and timely stories about your school. Make these forms available to teachers, students, and parents. If you have a news coordinator in your school system, start sending this individual those items that would attract media coverage.

With the information you provide, your system level news coordinator can now develop news releases and channel them to the appropriate media person. If you don't have a news coordinator, then it's up to you to find a way to write these news releases about your school. You can also use the news notes to generate stories for your monthly school newsletters. Open up the file "News" and scroll down to C5-3. Revise the sample to reflect your school.

FROM NEWS NOTE TO PRESS RELEASE

Based on the information given to you in a news note, you can now write a press release. Just remember to answer the 5 W's. Here's a sample to consider:

TEMPLATE C5-4. PRESS RELEASE

DAWSON COUNTY SCHOOL DISTRICT
Beth Thompson
Principal and Press Contact
Tel: 778-345-7878

SENIOR CITIZENS CATCH THE BEAT
WITH SCHOOL JAZZ TEAM

Sixth, seventh, and eighth graders from Mabry Middle School will help bring holiday cheer for local senior citizens with a dance exhibition scheduled for 2:00 p.m. Friday, December 15, at the Twin Towers Community Center.

The jazz fest will feature holiday songs and dances from around the world. Jane Ryan, a leg amputee, will perform a special solo number.

The dance exhibition is free and open to the public. The students will serve refreshments after the performance.

TOP-NOTCH NEWSLETTERS

Have you ever considered the notion that the majority of your parents never meet you face-to-face? Therefore, the only way they get to know you and the school is through the eyes of students and the words you deliver. This makes regular and informative home-school communication a major public relations tool. School newsletters, according to Pawlas (1995), can help you do the following:

♦ Provide accurate information about school programs, activities, and events.

♦ Build support for teachers, students, and school aims and objectives.

♦ Increase parent and community involvement in school activities.

♦ Involve parents in the teaching-learning process.

♦ Convey your professional beliefs about the educational process and how the school conducts business.

Principals who have developed top-notch newsletters usually establish a predictable format for sharing specific information about the school community. For example, they often include a section in which they feature comments from themselves about an issue or concern. Details highlighting student and teacher achievements are always included along with notification about interesting events and activities. Often a calendar of events is outlined to help keep parents informed of upcoming events and report grading dates. Here are several do's and don'ts for producing a top-notch school newsletter.

DOS AND DON'TS FOR TOP-NOTCH NEWSLETTERS

♦ Be selective about the material that's included. Unlike most printed materials, the school newsletter is read by most parents. Studies show that parents rate the school newsletter as an important data source about the school. Know your newsletter objectives: to inform, educate, and promote. Develop your newsletter content carefully and systematically.

- <u>Mention lots of people and mention them by name</u>: Students, staff, parents, and community members. Keep the newsletter focused on people and activities of the school. Resist the urge to use it as a soapbox.

- <u>Use the newsletter to keep your school community informed of school programs and events</u>. Done effectively, the school newsletter is a valuable public relations tool for you and your school.

- <u>Make your newsletter attractive and easy to read</u>. Your computer software program can really help you do this. You can save time by creating your newsletter from "document wizards" that most software programs now offer. These tools take you through the process of developing a wide variety of writing forms.

- <u>Keep the writing style consistent and conversational</u>. Use plain and familiar words. Keep sentences and paragraphs short.

- <u>Create a lively format</u>. Collect interesting quotations, pictures, and short articles that can be used. Interject humor.

- <u>Decide on a publication schedule and meet it</u>! Once the distribution schedule is determined, communicate this information to parents so they know when to expect it.

- <u>Devise a way to verify that parents get each issue</u>.

- <u>Review other school newsletters for additional ideas on format and content</u>.

Adapted from George Pawlas. *The Administrator's Guide to School Community Relations* (1995). Eye On Education Publisher: Princeton, NJ, pp. 135-157.

Here are disguised pages from a high school newsletter. We think the principal has done all the right things in producing a top-notch newsletter. Specifically, she has involved parents, teachers, and students in developing and distributing the newsletter. This communication tool has been collaboratively produced by members of all stakeholders.

We have reformatted the newsletter using a template wizard from our Microsoft Office software to show you how these tools can help you create these documents. Template C5-5 Newsletter follows.

Let's Chat

CONGRATULATIONS
HONOR ROLL
STUDENTS

Sophomores, Juniors, and Seniors sporting a 3.5 grade point average or better enjoyed an Honor Roll Breakfast hosted by the PTSA on October 5th and 6th in the school cafeteria.

Special thanks go to Mike Johnson, Kroger Bakery Manager, who helped even on his day off to ensure our students had a lasting supply of fresh doughnuts. Also, many thanks to Sharon Stone for donating yellow roses for table decorations. Great support and service from our own cafeteria staff made this a successful event.

We would also like to recognize the following PTSA volunteers who assisted in the preparation and hosting of the HONOR ROLL BREAKFAST:

Joan Reed, Sue Morris, Robert Drake, Ann Harris, Judy Lord, and Rose Mitchell.

The WHS PTSA thinks our Honor Roll Students are Super!

IMPORTANT DATES

NOVEMBER

5 Staff-Picture Makeup Day

11 PTSA Executive Board Meeting

12 Trade-Off Tuesday

27-29 School Closed

DECEMBER

2 Teacher Work Day

4 World AIDS Day

9 PTSA General Meeting and Holiday Concert

16 WHS Booster Club

18 Project Graduation Fund-Raiser Picture With Santa

23 Winter Holidays Begin

INSIDE

Let's Chat Newsletter

Published eight times a year
for parents, students,
teachers, and staff of WHS
PTSA

Windward High School
4578 Windward Road
Somewhere, USA

Principal
Linda Benson, Ph.D.

PTSA Co-Presidents
Gale Morris; Ann Lowe

PTSA Vice Presidents
for Community Relations
Tom Jones; Dee Hall

Newsletter Editors
Bill Weaver; Dee Hall

Proofreaders
Claire Cook; Jan Moore

Distribution
Tom Jones; Barb Burk

**Submit articles to the PTSA
mailbox at WHS. All articles
must have contact name
and phone number.
Please submit articles on a
computer diskette if
possible.
Thank you.**

Next Issue Deadline:
November 9, 19__

LEGISLATIVE ALERT

Re-Budgeting Process Begins

It's that time again when the Chairman of the County Commission, Bob Brown, the County Manager, Richard Denning, and the County Finance Director, Mark Channing, start preparing the budget for 19__.

It is important that we as parents in the Windward school community take every opportunity to attend public budget hearings.

WHY? We need to make sure the 10 million dollar Roads Program continues now and in the future. We fought for this program to make our streets safer and to reduce traffic congestion near our homes and schools.

MARK YOUR CALENDAR NOW. There will be a general forum on **November 14** at 8:00 p.m. in the Peachtree Fire Station. The Final Hearing is slated for **January 8, 19__** at 10:00 a.m. in the County Government Center.

BE THERE. We need good attendance at these meetings. Last year your support and attendance at these meetings and our campaign to write, call, or fax all county commissioners, helped to secure the 10 million for the Roads Program. Let's do it again this year.

Remember: When 3,000 households speak as one voice, elected officials LISTEN!

Have a question? Call Ann Lowe.

770/367-3434

On Your Payroll

The United States Senate

The Honorable Paul Dell
204 Russell Office Building
Washington, DC 20510
Tel: 202-224-2345

U.S. House of Representatives

The Honorable Tom Smith
Congressional District #5
2428 Rayburn House Building
Washington, DC 20515
Tel: 202-225-1234

The State Senate

Senator John Denton
999 Peachtree Street NE
Atlanta, GA 30309
Tel: 404-656-2323

Your County School Board

Glenda Bixby　Allen Paterson
Linda Hartman　Frank Markwell
Max McPherson　Betty Johns
Nancy McCormick

FROM THE PRINCIPAL'S DESK

Dear Parents:

Have you ever doubted your teen's horror stories of their school day? Ever wondered if classes really can be that boring or too hard? Are the halls really too crowded to get to class on time?

Here's an opportunity to find out for yourself.

Participate in Windward's first
TRADE-OFF TUESDAY
on November 12th.

It's a chance for parents and teens to trade places and experience each others' lives for a day. You've heard the saying, "If you want to understand someone, walk a mile in his shoes." Now is your chance to do it. We think you will gain a better understanding of your teen's point of view if you participate in this most unusual event. This day will turn back the clock and return you to your teenage years.

Here's how it works:

Parents, you attend school. Your teen does not! You must attend all classes for your student to be counted present for the day. If you cannot stay the entire day, the other parent can take your place or your teen must return to school.

- We encourage you to arrange for your teen to do your job. Your teen may accompany one parent to work while the other parent attends classes. Let your teen experience the "world of work" by doing your job while you do his or hers.

- You are expected to take notes and to "teach" basic material from each class to your teen.

- You may ride the school bus; however, we will work out parking arrangements should you drive.

I hope you will be able to arrange your calendar and place of business for this special event. It promises to be one of those rare opportunities whereby everybody wins. Watch for details on how to participate!

Sincerely,

Linda Benson
Principal

For Your Information

The Learning Channel
is proud to present

Parent Connection

This special program focuses on the importance of parental involvement in children's education.

Tune in on Sunday, October 27th, 12:00 to 12:30 EST

SPOTLIGHT ON SPORTS

Softball Team Memorializes Former Teammate

Jane Carey
10th Grade Student Staff Reporter

The WHS Softball Team dedicates this season to the memory of their friend and teammate, Barbara Bass.

A colorful embroidered patch in the design of a softball will be worn on the right sleeve of the Varsity uniforms. The design of the patch includes the initials "BB" and her playing number "15" over the top of a multicolored rainbow.

The artwork was suggested by Barbara's art teacher, Ms. Judy Bazemore, and was inspired by Barbara's own drawings. The rainbow speaks to one of Barbara's hopes for the future-equality. There was no place for prejudice or any other type of mistreatment as she saw it, and she spoke often about it with her family and friends.

Barbara didn't just speak of equality--she felt a personal responsibility to live it, and did so. This is her legacy.

Mrs. Margaret Mason, a friend and WHS parent, took the artwork and made the patches. She asked the Lady Cougars to accept the patches as a gift from her to Barbara's memory.

Barbara was a member of the first Lady Cougars Fastpitch Softball Team last year. Her jersey number 15 has been retired and will be framed and displayed.

Barbara was killed in a traffic accident while on summer vacation. We will miss her.

CHEERLEADING SQUAD SHOOTS FOR FIRST PLACE

The WHS Varsity Cheerleading Squad ranks 2nd in their region and 5th in the state after last year's busy season. Mary Martin, squad coach states, " We're shooting for first in the State this year."

The girls practice three days a week for six hours, cheer at the games on Friday, and most of them are also practicing hard on an outside All-Star squad several hours a week.

Along with cheering and competing, the girls are expected to keep up their grades in school and be good role models to other students.

The team's first cheer-leading competition will be held at North Central on November 23rd. Come on over and watch a great team. They are awesome!

WHS WELCOMES NEW BASKETBALL COACH

Mark Harmon

9th Grade Student Staff Reporter

Mr. Brian Hill accepts coaching position at WHS. Coach Hill has a Master's Degree in Health and Physical Education and ten years of playing and coaching experience .

Our best wishes for a good season.

FROM THE COUNSELING CORNER

Attention Ninth Grade Parents

A special meeting is planned for all ninth grade parents. The Counseling Office will host a meeting for parents on Tuesday, **November 19, 19__** to cover a variety of topics related to **student academic success.**

Meet with us at 7:30 p.m. in the cafeteria to hear about changes in the **HOPE Scholarship qualifications** and new **diploma options** for the class of 2000.

Other topics:

- **Study Skills**
- **Homework Hotline**
- **Weekly Progress Reports**
- **Testing**
- **Long-Range Guidance Program**
- **Parent Involvement in Student Success**

Plan For Success Student Seminars

Learn how to plan for success by attending weekly study skills seminars each Monday, during the first half of each lunch period in the Counseling Suite.

You will learn how to apply methods and skills that lead to academic success in school. Students who give at least 25 minutes, once each week, find their attitude and grades start to soar.

If you plan to learn then you must learn to plan.

Topics for Winter:

- **Getting Organized**
- **Setting Realistic Goals**
- **Jogging Your Memory Bank**
- **Surviving the Test**
- **Scheduling Long-Term Projects**
- **Prioritizing Your Homework**

FOR YOUR INFORMATION

Multicultural Task Force Committee, headed by assistant principal James Ford, along with two counselors and four teachers is in the process of starting a peer mediation program at WHS. Thirty selected tenth graders will be trained as mediators in November. Students will learn conflict-solving strategies.

The Differential Aptitude Test (DAT) and Career Interest Inventory will be given to all ninth graders on October 23 and 24. The results of these tests can be helpful in future course selection and college planning. Results will be mailed home later in the year and we encourage you to review them with your student's counselor.

Career Day is scheduled for February 26, 19__. Any parent interested in participating should contact Kathy Cline in the Counseling Office.

FACULTY FOOTNOTES

The ABC's of Success

**Luke Larson & Jill Reeves
PE Department**

- Be on time and in your seat when the bell rings.

- Care about your fellow man, and he'll care about you.

- Direction and focus are the keys to success.

- Guarantee you will give your best effort.

- Interest in your own success contributes to success.

**Alycia Wells & Bill Phillips
Math Department**

- Join a club or committee. Active students seem to budget their time better.

- Keep track of all assignments on a calendar.

- Learn by doing, not by just listening.

**Alison Black & Trish Hall
Science Department**

- Study a little bit each night.

- Teach someone else the material; it is the best

way to make sure you know it.

- Volunteer for extra credit work.

- Xerox a classmate's notes if you are absent.

- Catching zzz's is better at night than in class. Get your rest.

GET SMART

A study room, staffed by a certified teacher, is available for students' use during all five lunch periods. Parents may want to encourage their students to make use of this resource located in Room 345.

Students can read, do homework, make study aids, etc., and receive academic help in the study room.

Making use of this quiet, quality study time should be especially valuable to students who have after-school commitments and demands on their time.

Peers Helping Peers

Linda Blair
Faculty Sponsor

As one of the sponsors of the National Honor Society, I help supervise the club's service project, peer tutoring.

Students from WHS who are having academic difficulty can request a tutor through WHS. The request can be made to Beth Hanson or Tony Bianco, tutorial student chair-persons.

The student will then be matched with an WHS National Honor Society club member and will then meet with the tutor at a mutually agreeable time and place.

The cost of the service, $5.00 per hour, will go to WHS Project Graduation Fund.

Exercise C5-3
SIZING UP YOUR SCHOOL NEWSLETTER

Pull out copies of your school newsletter. Using the Dos and Don'ts listed in the training module, rate your publication. What will you do differently? How did the sample newsletter from a colleague help you?

REFERENCES

Brigham, N. (1991). *How to do leaflets, newsletters & newspapers*. Detroit, MI: PEP Publishers.

Joyce, A. (1991). *Written communications and the school administrator*. Boston, MA: Allyn and Bacon.

Pawlas, G. (1995) *The administrator's guide to school-community relations*. Princeton, NJ: Eye On Education.

Pawlas, G., and Meyers, K. (1989). *The principal and communication*. Bloomington, IN: Elementary Principal Series No. 3. Phi Delta Kappa Educational Foundation.

Vann, A. (1992). *Ten ways to improve principal-parent communication, Principal, 71* (3), 30-31.

RESOURCES

Vendor: North Light Clip Art Series
       1507 Dana Ave.
       Cincinnati, OH 45207
       Tel: 1-800-289-0963

North Light offers a diverse selection of clip art that can be used in school publications with no copyright infringement.

Vendor: Corel Corp.
       P.O. Box 3595
       Salinas, CA 93912-3595
       Tel: 613-728-8200

Corel provides a volume of clip art that can be used in school publications with no copyright infringement.

COMPETENCY SIX

BROCHURES, BULLETINS, FLYERS, AND POSTERS

COMPETENCY STATEMENT

Design informative special communications from the school to advertise, publicize, or seek support for teachers, students, and school programs.

KNOWLEDGE BASE HIGHLIGHTS

Podsen 1991. Memo and letter writing are the most frequently used forms of written communication. Principals write least often types of writing directed toward mass communication to parents, students, and the general community (i.e., questionnaires, brochures, bulletins, news releases, and newsletters).

Brigham 1991. "A brochure is a glorified leaflet. It is a short, often urgent written message that should cause a reader to stop dead in his tracks to read it."

IT PAYS TO ADVERTISE

You have an important open house to announce, need to get the facts out to head off a rumor, or want to rally support for a school fund raiser. What you need is a *brochure, flyer, poster,* or *bulletin.*

Communicating with the school's external audiences is not a communication strategy used systematically and frequently by principals (Podsen, 1991). Therefore, writing forms such as brochures, bulletins, and flyers are not developed often. However, in today's world principals need to "advertise to the community" what is going on in the school (Pawlas, 1995). If you don't take care of a potential supporter or critic, someone else will!

WHO ARE YOUR EXTERNAL AUDIENCES?

Taxpayers	Teachers Union	Businesses
Service Clubs	Preschool Parents	Industry
Civic Groups	Ethnic Groups	Retired Citizens
Legislators	Churches	Single adults

Take a few moments to think about these various audiences. Picture the typical reader in a particular audience; however, don't make assumptions about family status, jobs, age, attitudes, education, and racial, ethnic and gender groups.

WHAT DO THEY WANT TO KNOW?

Generally, these individuals want to know how students are performing and behaving. Each audience will want to know more about a particular aspect of the school but each is concerned how the quality of the school will impact on them.

HOW CAN YOU TELL THEM?

People in our general community need to know about our schools. However, they don't need an annual report. Brochures, bulletins, flyers, and posters are quick and effective tools for principals to use to accomplish a specific purpose for a targeted audience. These are short written messages posted on bulletin boards, handed out at PTA meetings, or included in real estate informational packets.

DESIGNING YOUR ADVERTISING TOOLS

These focused messages must capture the reader's attention FAST. Something at the top needs to pull the reader closer after a quick glance. Nancy Brigham (1991) gives us five tips to get started.

TARGET YOUR AUDIENCE AND PURPOSE

Think about the typical parent, businessman, grocery clerk, or senior citizen you want to tell about the school. Target the purpose of your message. Do you want to inform, persuade, call to action, seek support, or brag about a recent school achievement? All these things will influence how you shape and present your message. If you have a school advisory council with broad community representation, use them to plan and edit these publications. Their reactions will reflect the subtleties of how various groups think.

LIST YOUR IDEAS; THEN FOCUS ON A KEY ISSUE OR THEME

Put all your ideas down by listing them, or outlining them, or drawing a mindmap. What do you want to say? Review your ideas and circle the ones that will appeal most to your audience. Look for a theme or one compelling idea to draw the reader.

WRITE A SNAZZY HEADLINE

The headline must snare the reader. The reader wants to know, how will this relate to me? Time for most readers is scarce.

GRAB ATTENTION WITH GRAPHICS OR PICTURES

Brigham (1991, p. 101) tells us that "big, striking pictures and photos attract readers." Graphics help the reader visualize the information in the brochure or bulletin. More important, a good picture "dramatizes an idea" and requires less text. She sums it up this way: "An article written partly with pictures is shorter, quicker to read, more powerful, and more fun to look at than a page full of words."

MAKE THE MESSAGE VISIBLE

Use varying font sizes and styles to keep the text easy to read. Show lots of white space. No brochure or flyer should be "jam-packed" with words. Highlight important phrases or the central message. Keep the message easily accessible to the reader by using headings and subheadings.

TEMPLATE C6-1. BROCHURE FOR PTA MEMBERSHIP
PURPOSE: TO PERSUADE
AUDIENCE: PARENTS AND TEACHERS
TONE: COLLABORATIVE

Document Analysis

THE HOME-SCHOOL ADVANTAGE

Dear Parents and Teachers:

Each year we come together to guide our students into the future.

In 96-97, our theme was **Be All You Can Be: Set Your Mind On It!**

Vary font sizes and styles.

In 97-98, we're still thinking *Be All You Can Be*. But our community of learners is moving forward. That's reflected in our current theme:

BE ALL YOU CAN BE:
TH*I*NK COMM*U*N*I*TY

Grab attention with graphics.

We believe *Be All You Can Be: Think Community* is a timely theme for our school.

Like our world, our community is growing, changing, and moving. As our community changes, our school changes. And as our schools, so do our students and parents.

Show lots of white space.

In a rapidly changing world, our students need parents and teachers working together to build a better community of support for our future leaders—our students.

Your Parent-Teacher-Student Association needs you!

**Join your PTSA today.
And make a difference tomorrow!**

Make your message visible.

HIGH SCHOOL
OPEN HOUSE GET TOGETHER
October 15
7:00-9:00 p.m.
School Media Center

To **THINK** you need **BRAINS**

To **SEE** you need **EYES**

To **MOVE** you need *CALORIES*

To **SUCCEED** you need

DR*IV*E

Document Analysis

Highlight important information.

Grab attention with graphics.

Use highlighting techniques.

Success in school as in all areas of life is not a matter of luck, but comes about through planning.

Come to our **OPEN HOUSE** on **October 15** and learn how we can work together to help your teenager **plan for success.** After a short session in the media center, you will follow your teen's academic schedule. Our challenge as teachers and parents is to help each student set learning goals and to work toward them by:

Appeal to the parents' need to see school, meet teachers, learn more about program.

Setting realistic goals.
Dreams are always encouraged.

Setting reasonable time limits.
Time for fun is always negotiable!

Energizing your mind.
We know the body works!

The writer uses humor to keep reader's interest.

Drafting a plan.
What-Why-When- and HOW!

Visualizing success.
It really is mind over matter!

Rewarding yourself when you accomplish a goal.
A new car? Go back to step one!!

TEMPLATE C6-3. SPECIAL PURPOSE BULLETIN

SPECIAL BULLETIN

MT. PARK ELEMENTARY SCHOOL

1997
SCHOOL OF EXCELLENCE

- Accolades came to Mt. Park Elementary School from the State Superintendent John Lane as he announced the 1997 State Schools of Excellence. Mt. Park now qualifies for the national Blue Ribbon Schools Program next year. Recipients of this award are selected from criteria that include student focus, quality of instruction and academic standards, school-family partnerships, awards and other honors received, obstacles overcome, and quality of long-range planning.

- Superintendent Lane stated, " To be selected as a State School of Excellence is the highest honor our public schools can enjoy. To be selected means the highest level of commitment from everyone involved with a school, from students and teachers to administrators, parents, and community leaders. These schools are living examples of our highest hopes for education."

Mt. Park Elementary is an example of a school and community working together to provide excellence in education.

Document Analysis

Uses graphics to attract reader's attention.

Varies font size and type.

Highlights key points.

Provides additional information.

Gives praise to all stakeholders.

Exercise C6-1
IT's YOUR TURN

Think about a school program you would like to publicize to your local community. Follow these steps in designing your brochure.

♦ Complete the Action Planning Sheet and note your starting time in beginning this writing task.

Action Planning Sheet

Starting Time:_____

What is my purpose in writing this brochure?

Who is my audience?

What is the attitude of this audience? Positive/Neutral/Negative?

What information do they need?

What tone do I want to convey?

♦ Map your ideas before you write. You can make a list, an outline, or a mindmap. The point is to put all your ideas down on paper.

Getting Started

Once you have targeted your purpose and audience, list all your ideas. Do not edit or evaluate. Just get all your ideas down on paper.

1. **List the main ideas about your program.**
2. **Select the key points.**
3. **Turn each key point into a headline.**
4. **Support each headline with the most important details.**

♦ Select an organizational strategy. Refer to page 17 which outlines the ways you can structure the message. Which one will you use?

♦ Now draft your brochure. Insert your disk and open file C6-4. Copy the template and draft your brochure.

♦ Check with your local office supply companies. You can create a professional look with complete ensembles of coordinated stationery to produce the following:

Letterheads	Business Cards	Awards
Signs	Tri-fold Brochures	Flyers
Announcements	Message Papers	Bulletins
Invitations	Newsletters	

Template C6-4. Brochure
Three-Column Format

Program Highlights

- _____
  _____
  _____
  _____
  _____

- _____
  _____
  _____
  _____
  _____

- _____
  _____
  _____
  _____

Name and Address of School

Insert Title or Caption

Insert Graphic or Picture

Central Theme or Message

Graphic
or
Photo

Major Heading,
Graphic or
Photo

SUMMARY

Being recognized as an effective leader requires more than the sign on the door or the title on your desk. Influencing others is a critical skill in today's workplace where you must interact with many school critics and supporters. Looking ahead into the twenty-first century, principals will continue to need public support to endorse school initiatives. One of the many ways to win support from others is to systematically promote school achievements and programs through brochures, flyers, and other marketing tools.

REFERENCES

Brigham, N. (1991) *How to do leaflets, newsletters & newspapers.* Detroit, MI: PEP Publishers.

Pawlas, G. (1995). *The administrator's guide to school-community relations.* Princeton, NJ: Eye On Education.

Podsen, I. (1991). Apprehension and effective writing in the principalship. *NASSP Bulletin 75* (532) 89-96.

RESOURCES

Vendor: North Light Clip Art Series
      1507 Dana Ave.
      Cincinnati, OH 45207
      Tel: 1-800-289-0963

North Light offers a diverse selection of clip art that can be used in school publications with no copyright infringement.

Vendor: Corel Corp.
      P.O. Box 3595
      Salinas, CA 93912-3595
      Tel: 613-728-8200

Corel provides a volume of clip art that can be used in school publications with no copyright infringement.

COMPETENCY SEVEN

SURVEYS AND QUESTIONNAIRES

COMPETENCY STATEMENT

Develop two-way written communication tools that invite stakeholders to share their thoughts, ideas, and feelings about school-centered issues, concerns, or problems.

KNOWLEDGE BASE HIGHLIGHTS

Hoyle, English, & Steffy 1990. "The most scientific way to determine the public's perception of school issues is to conduct a survey of the community and staff. However, informal telephone calls as well as questionnaires in school newsletters can yield interesting information. Building support for schools requires a systematic public relations plan."

Pankake, Stewart, & Winn 1990. "School leaders who are effective communicators recognize that communication is a two-way process. Principals who understand this idea do more than just send messages; they are interested in receiving as well."

Tewel 1990. Astute principals establish clear, comprehensive, and valid channels of communication with the school community by assessing the human realities of the school organization. Surveys are good ways to gather these data.

Howlett 1993. Political acumen has become a survival skill for school leaders. School administrators can orchestrate community effort and support by establishing effective public relations programs.

Pawlas 1995. "While it is essential to tell the public about the school, it is also incumbent upon a principal to listen to the public's response to information and, after serious examination, to use the feedback to improve future communication."

SEEKING DIFFERING VIEWPOINTS

Approachable leaders are more likely to be informed of both negative and positive information. No one likes surprises. By seeking information and being open to differing viewpoints you achieve two goals. First, you communicate that the ideas and opinions of others are valuable and helpful. Second, you get feedback about what's going on in the school. As a school leader you need to resist the tendency to perceive only what you want to see. Two-way communication tools can help you avoid near-sightedness.

Surveys, questionnaires, polls, and interviews administered to school community groups can provide valuable data sources. Here are four reasons to use these tools on a regular basis.

- ♦ Attitudes of parents, teachers, students, and general community members provide data to support conclusions and recommendations about the school program. This type of information strengthens annual reports.

- ♦ As schools change and grow, it becomes necessary to make sure current programs are still meeting the needs of all members of the learning community. Surveys and questionnaires can be used to assess current effectiveness or the need for updating or replacing a program.

- ♦ In today's world principals who write grant proposals increase the chance of securing outside funding and resources for teaching and learning needs in their schools. Survey data can be used in these proposals to establish need or to describe school/community attitudes, opinions, and support.

- ♦ Perception soon becomes the reality of a situation. School leaders need accurate and frank evaluations of school programs as the members of various community groups see them.

Developing written questionnaires requires time to plan, write, administer, and interpret the results. The major writing task is to construct clear and concise survey questions.

TIPS FOR WRITING SURVEY QUESTIONS

♦ Write your purpose statement. Example: *I intend to find out if WHO are satisfied with WHAT.*

♦ Brainstorm a list of all the questions you want to answer.

♦ Review the list and eliminate any questions that do not support your purpose statement.

♦ Decide on the response format to your questions. Open-ended questions allow respondents to write their answers and therefore provide additional information. Structured response items ask participants to choose between or among a limited number of choices. You may force a choice between two or three responses, such as: *Yes* or *No* or *Agree, Uncertain,* or *Disagree*

♦ Review program goals and objectives before writing questions. They may suggest to you several possible ideas for questions.

♦ Assess the audience and reading levels of participants. Your computer program may have a readability index to help you determine reading levels.

♦ Limit the number of questions to about 25 items. Keep it reasonable on the time demand of your reader.

♦ Arrange the questions in some logical order. Avoid asking the same question twice.

♦ Write clear directions on how and when to complete the survey. A cover letter explaining the need for this information and how it will benefit the school might put your reader in a receptive mood.

♦ Make the survey attractive and very readable. Use wide margins; edit carefully for grammatical errors; and make it visually appealing.

Adapted from Joyce, A. (1991). *Written Communications and the School Administrator.* Boston, MA: Allyn and Bacon, pp. 147-154.

SAMPLE SURVEYS

On the following pages we offer three surveys/questionnaires that reflect the suggestions above. What do you think?

TEMPLATE C7-1. FORCED CHOICE FORMAT
STUDENT QUESTIONNAIRE

Please check the box that describes you best.	Most of the time	Half of the time	Not very often
Understands Teaching Goals/Objectives.			
• I know the purpose for each lesson.			
• I understand the homework assignments.			
• I understand the directions given in class.			
Actively Engaged			
• I raise my hand a lot to answer questions.			
• I get to share my ideas in class with other students.			
• Sometimes I work alone and in small groups.			
Relates to Student			
• The things I learn are useful to me outside of class.			
• I am asked to seek information or materials from outside the schools to use in class work.			
• I can select topics to study that I like.			
Feels Successful			
• I feel good about coming to school.			
• I think I am learning a lot.			
• I feel I am successful in most subjects.			
Plans for Learning			
• I set my own learning goals.			
• I develop a plan to reach my learning goals.			
• My teachers help me to reach my learning goals.			
• Tests and assignments help me to know how well I have learned or practiced.			

Orderly Classroom			
• I understand the class rules.			
• I feel the rules are fair.			
• The teacher enforces the rules fairly.			
• I helped establish the class rules.			
• The students in class follow the rules.			
Peer Interaction			
• I have friends in school.			
• The students in this class help each other.			
• Other students seem to like me.			

TEMPLATE C7-2. OPEN-ENDED FORMAT
PARENT SURVEY

Dear Parents:

Your comments and suggestions are needed. We want to make sure we are doing everything possible to make our school the best it can be. Please complete the questionnaire and return it to the school by January 15. Thank you.

1. My child's overall attitude toward school is _____

_____

2. My child's attitude toward his/her teacher is _____

_____

3. My child worries most about _____

_____

4. As a parent I am concerned most about _____

_____

5. An area I would like to see my child experience success in is _____

_____

6. Please list the positive things you like best about our school:

_____

7. Please list the things you would like to see the school improve upon.

_____

_____

8. What are some things you have wondered about or heard about that you would like more information on?

_____

_____

_____

9. Do you think the school program is meeting the needs of students?

_____

_____

_____

10. What ideas do you have to improve our school?

_____

_____

_____

11. How would you rate our overall effectiveness as a school?

Thank you for taking time to complete this questionnaire.

TEMPLATE C7-3. COMBINATION FORMAT
STAFF SURVEY

Directions to Staff: What follows is a survey to determine your perception of how productively our school functions in areas considered to be essential for school success. Current information about our work behaviors will help us to develop our capacity to improve both our professional interactions and student successes. Please respond to each item as follows: *Agree (A), Not Sure (NS),* or *Disagree (D).* In the COMMENT SECTION please elaborate on any idea or concern you have in this area. Thank you for your help.

	A	NS	D
SCHOOL PLANNING			
1. We develop school improvement goals and objectives each year.			
2. School improvement goals and objectives should be the framework for assessing our school.			
3. The staff should be involved in gathering and analyzing data about school improvement goals.			
4. The staff does not need to be involved in setting school goals.			
5. Staff members need to express concerns about school-centered problems through a systematic process.			
6. Representatives from parent, student, and general community groups should be included in the development of school wide goals and objectives.			
7. A relationship should exist between school goals and staff work activities.			
8. A relationship should exist between school goals and staff work activities.			
COMMENTS			

TEACHER EVALUATION	A	NS	D
1. Teachers need regular feedback on their teaching performance.			
2. Teacher assessment should include a preobservation conference, observation, data collection, and a feedback conference.			
3. Teachers should observe and coach one another.			
4. Teachers should be supervised for enhancing and improving their instructional skills.			
5. Video taped lessons are productive tools for self-assessment.			
COMMENTS			

WORK GROUP PERFORMANCE	A	NS	D
1. The leadership team should identify teaching teams, work assignments, and committees.			
2. Staff work groups identify meeting goals and objectives.			
3. Staff members generally do not work well in groups.			
4. Staff members should have input into teaching assignments and committee work.			
5. Each work group selects a team leader to help define group tasks, time lines, and responsibilities.			
6. Work groups should assess the quality of group interaction and task assigned.			
7. All members of the group participate.			
8. The principal needs to intervene when work groups become unproductive.			
9. Work groups should report to principal on progress, results, and future plans.			
10. The principal should review and critique the performance of work groups or teams.			

11.Staff needs assistance in shared decision making and group work skills.			
COMMENTS			
STAFF DEVELOPMENT	**A**	**NS**	**D**
1. School goals and objectives should relate to the school's staff development program.			
2. Teachers are involved in designing and implementing the school's staff development program.			
3. Staff development should reflect teacher concerns, not research on effective teaching and learning.			
4. Teachers need to develop new instructional materials regularly.			
5. Inservice programs reflect best practices about adult learning.			
6. Staff development program should provide opportunities to practice new skills.			
COMMENTS			
INSTRUCTIONAL PROGRAM	**A**	**NS**	**D**
1. Teachers use both national and local curriculum standards to guide instructional planning.			
2. Instruction is planned around the assessed needs of the learners.			
3. Instructional planning is integrated across teachers and subjects.			

4. Students know the learning objective for each lesson.			
5. Students are actively engaged in the learning.			
6. Students participate in establishing learning goals and objectives.			
7. Teachers provide students with feedback on their learning performance through a variety of assessment tools.			
8. Teachers manage classroom disruptions with low level intervention techniques.			
9. The staff knows the developmental characteristics of the learners and uses this knowledge to design effective learning situations.			
COMMENTS			

SCHOOL ASSESSMENT OF OUTCOMES	A	NS	D
1. School evaluation should be examined on the results of the school's performance on targeted goals and objectives.			
2. Individual staff members assess themselves based on their performance goals and objectives.			
3. Work groups should conduct a formal evaluation.			
4. Staff evaluation is based on a variety of data and observations.			
5. Student evaluation is based on specific measures of achievement in a variety of areas.			
6. Teachers should evaluate the extent to which the principal facilitates staff productivity.			
COMMENTS			

Adapted from Karolyn Snyder's "Personal Perception Profile on Productive School Management." In *Managing Productive Schools*, Harcourt Brace Jovanovich, 1988, pp. 19-25.

TEMPLATE C7-4. CREATIVE FORMAT
STAFF-PRINCIPAL RELATIONSHIP EVALUATION

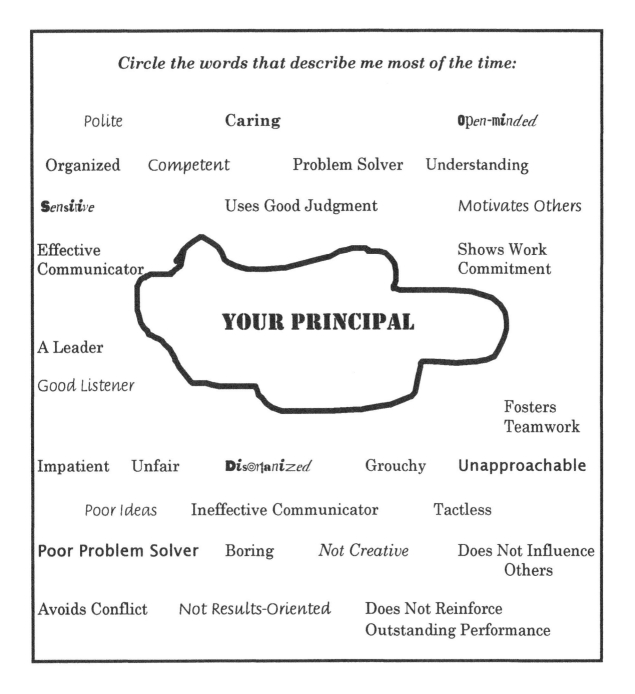

Circle the words that describe me most of the time:

Polite   Caring   Open-minded

Organized   Competent   Problem Solver   Understanding

Sensitive   Uses Good Judgment   Motivates Others

Effective   Shows Work
Communicator   Commitment

YOUR PRINCIPAL

A Leader

Good Listener

Fosters
Teamwork

Impatient   Unfair   Disorganized   Grouchy   Unapproachable

Poor Ideas   Ineffective Communicator   Tactless

Poor Problem Solver   Boring   Not Creative   Does Not Influence
Others

Avoids Conflict   Not Results-Oriented   Does Not Reinforce
Outstanding Performance

Exercise C7-1
It's Your Turn

School-Community Education Survey

Using the suggestions and templates presented in this training module, develop a survey targeted toward a specific audience. Find examples of surveys and questionnaires that are eye-catching and easy to read. Model their lead.

Summary

As a school leader you cannot depend solely upon your observations, opinions, and views about school matters. You will need to have current and timely data about all aspects of the school if you are to show competence in managing the financial and qualitative aspects of your job. Successful programs and ongoing improvement require measurement. Effective school principals find ways to assess both the tangibles and the intangibles within the school community. They look in from both the inside and the outside, making sure that all stakeholders, internal and external, are part of this analysis.

References

Hoyle, J., English, F., and Steffy, B. (1990). *Skills for successful school leaders*. Arlington, VA: American Association of School Administrators.

Howlett, P. (January, 1993). Politics comes to school. *Executive Educator, 15* (1), 111-120.

Pankake, A., et al. (November, 1990). Choices for effective communication: Which channels to use. *NASSP Bulletin, 74* (529), 53-57.

Pawlas, G. (1995). *The administrator's guide to school-community relations*. Princeton, NJ: Eye On Education.

Tewel, K. (March, 1990). Improving in-school communications: A technique for principals. *NASSP Bulletin, 74* (524), 39-41.

COMPETENCY EIGHT

GRADE A RESUMES

COMPETENCY STATEMENT

Engineer a compelling resume in order to present skills and results to various publics and for career changes.

KNOWLEDGE BASE HIGHLIGHTS

Simon 1981. "The most qualified people don't always get the job. It goes to the person who presents himself most persuasively in person and on paper."

Eyler 1990. "The preparation of a resume is a practical art—a delicate balance of things said and left unsaid, detail provided and information meaningfully summarized, the efficient use of space and the power of pleasing graphic effects."

Marino 1990. "Resumes should be designed so that the person involved in the resume screening process can look at the resume in a 30-second glance and decide to put it in the *YES* pile."

Anthony & Roe, 1994. "For educators, a resume is not only a job search tool: it is an ongoing record of professional development submitted for merit or tenure reviews, grant applications, or to support candidacy for leadership positions."

30 SECONDS IS ALL YOU GET

According to Tom Jackson (1990), "The perfect resume is not a biography or memoir.

It is a well-structured, easy to read presentation of your capabilities and accomplishments, designed to convince a potential employer to invite you for an interview" (p. 57). Thirty seconds is about all you get when a personnel manager scans your resume and either decides to pull you in for an interview or eliminate you as a contender. You may have years of experience and unique expertise, but if your resume sells you short, you won't even make the *maybe* pile.

Principals aspiring to another school setting, the central office, and even the superintendency need to know how to design an effective resume and cover letter. Your resume MUST project a professional image.

EDUCATORS NEED RESUMES

Times have changed. Perhaps when you first started your educational career a resume was not expected. You filled out an application and had an interview. However, federal and state legislation often requires school systems to advertise job vacancies in order to meet equal opportunity standards for all who seek these positions. When the number of qualified applicants exceeds the number of job vacancies, competition for these positions becomes the name of the game. According to Anthony and Roe (1994), a resume is an essential document for:

♦ student teachers

♦ first-year teachers

♦ experienced teachers

♦ substitute teachers

♦ paraprofessionals

♦ supervisors

♦ consultants

♦ principals

♦ superintendents

DIFFERENT STROKES FOR DIFFERENT FOLKS

There are numerous resume books and computer software packages that can assist you in this task when your career goals are changing. However, Anthony and Roe (1994) strongly suggest that the educator's resume "only superficially resembles the typical business model."

"Educators should not attempt to follow the dictates of other occupations. The focus, the emphasis, the vocabulary, and the overall message are different. The result will not strike the appropriate tone, nor will it focus on educational objectives. Educators do not have a product, educational progress is not always and not necessarily measured in percentages, promotion is hardly an issue, and profitability is not the bottom line" (p. 6).

SELF-PROMOTION IS NOT BRAGGING

Today's professional educator needs a resume for other reasons. As a school leader you are asked to make presentations to numerous community groups. Many principals become consultants to other school systems, sharing their expertise in a specific area. Quite often you may be asked to submit a resume so you can be introduced properly and accurately. In addition, if you are seeking an advisory position on a board or professional office in a state organization, you may be asked for a resume. Finally, if you ask a colleague for a letter of recommendation for a particular purpose, a copy your resume will help the writer be specific in describing your skills and abilities.

The bottom line is this: Principals must learn how to present their skills and abilities to their various publics. The challenge is to create a professionally appropriate resume, one that "reflects your culture" and promotes you as a "committed educator with experiences and abilities that produce results consistent with current practice and procedures" (Anthony & Roe, 1994).

RESUME WRITING DO'S AND DON'TS

THE DO'S

- ♦ Know your audience. Target the information needed to assist a decision in your favor.

- ♦ Keep sentences and paragraphs short. No more than 10 lines.

- ♦ Use indented and "bulleted" statements. Make use of dynamic action words such as created, analyzed, leveraged, restored, consolidated, invented, eliminated, expanded, implemented, etc.

- ♦ Use quantities, amounts, dollar values where they enhance the description of what you did ("Decreased student suspensions by 50 percent").

- ♦ Put strongest achievements first and then work downward.

- ♦ Include hobbies or social interests only if they relate to your current job target.

♦ Avoid self-evaluations. For example:

"I am an intelligent and resourceful administrator." Well, we are entitled to our opinion BUT

"Developed a $10,000 grant proposal for a dropout prevention program" states the facts and emphasizes RESULTS.

♦ Stress your ability to master new concepts, ideas, practices.

♦ Highlight your skills in organizing and reorganizing new data, work patterns, and processes.

♦ Capitalize on your ability to be entrepreneurial, results-focused, and multicultural.

♦ Emphasize your computer knowledge and your data-based communication skills.

THE DON'TS

♦ Don't include pictures. You may bear a striking resemblance to a least-liked relative.

♦ Don't list references. A potential employer is interested in references only after he or she considers you a strong contender.

♦ Don't list personal irrelevancies (height, weight, sex).

♦ Don't highlight personal problems.

♦ Don't stretch the truth.

♦ Don't make any written communication errors. Remember: your resume is an example of your ability to handle job correspondence.

♦ Don't write more than one or two pages. Provide an addendum to highlight additional accomplishments.

Adapted from Tom Jackson, *The Perfect Resume*, Doubleday Publishing, New York, 1990, pp. 63-64.

Adapted from Rebecca Anthony and Gerald Roe, *101 Grade A Resumes for Teachers*, Barron's Educational Series, New York, 1994, pp. 1-7.

RESUME SAMPLE FORMATS

TEMPLATE C8-1. CLUSTER/FUNCTIONAL/SKILLS-BASED FORMAT
PURPOSE: TO PERSUADE
AUDIENCE: PERSONNEL DIRECTOR
STRATEGY: TOPIC

SHAWN CAREY	**Document Analysis**
9845 Twingate Drive Callaway, VA 24567 540-468-2323 (Office) 540-468-1212 (Residence)	
JOB TARGET: ASSISTANT SUPERINTENDENT FOR CURRICULUM	Specifies job target.

EXECUTIVE SUMMARY

♦ Public school administrator with 10 years of administrative and 5 years of teaching experience.

♦ Significant budget, community relations, and unionized teacher management experience.

♦ Innovative instructional leadership approaches to teacher evaluation and student achievement.

Highlights key skills and experience.

COMPETENCIES

Administration

♦ Principal of a 2500 student, 125 certified staff public high school in a suburban setting.

♦ Assistant Principal of a 1000 student, 60 faculty and staff rural middle school.

Selects functional resume format to focus attention on competency areas specified in job announcement.

Budget

♦ Responsible for the preparation and management of a $6 million school budget.

♦ Planned and implemented a $1.5 million school renovation project.

Uses bullets and varies font size to highlight key information.

♦ Developed and received a $10,000 grant for student dropout prevention program.

Each point is made and supported with a specific, results-oriented focus.

Curriculum

♦ Designed a student dropout prevention program resulting in a 20 percent decrease in high school dropouts.

♦ Implemented computer-assisted math and reading programs.

Supervision

♦ Initiated a differentiated supervision approach to teacher evaluation. Trained master teachers and mentor teachers to assist in this process. Increased staff teaching skills resulted in higher staff morale and a steady rise in student achievement based on quarterly test results.

Community and Labor Relations

♦ Led successful bond drive in two communities resulting in major construction and renovation funding.

♦ Senior district representative for two school systems with successful no-strike negotiations concluded in both situations.

EXPERIENCE

Experience and degrees are essential parts to the resume but are stated last.

1985-Present:	Principal, Callaway High School, Callaway, VA.

1980-1985:	Assistant. Principal, Lindley Middle School, Milton, VA.

Attention is placed on competency areas.

1979-1980:	Team Curriculum Leader, Tremont High School, Patchogue, NY.

1978-1979:	Mathematics Teacher, Tremont High School, Patchogue, NY.

1975-1978:	Mathematics Teacher, South Ocean Junior High, Medford, NY.

EDUCATION

Master of Education (M.Ed.)
School Administration and Supervision
Central Virginia University, 1980

Bachelor of Science (BS)
Math/Physics Major
Stonybrook University, 1975

TEMPLATE C8-2. CHRONOLOGICAL/WORK HISTORY FORMAT

Shawn Carey

9845 Twingate Drive
Callaway, VA 24567
540-468-2323 (Office)
540-468-1212 (Home)

OBJECTIVE: Assistant Superintendent for Curriculum

EDUCATION:

♦ Harvard Principals Center, Boston, MA
  Principal-in-Residence Summer Program, 1996

♦ Central Virginia University, Roanoke, VA
  M.Ed. Educational Administration, 1980

♦ Stonybrook University, Happauge, NY
  BS Degree, Physics/Math, 1975
  Summa Cum Laude

ADMINISTRATIVE EXPERIENCE:

High School Principal, Callaway High School, Callaway, VA, 1985-Present.

♦ Principal of a 2500 student, 125 certified staff public high school in a suburban setting.

♦ Responsible for the preparation and management of a $6 million school budget.

Document Analysis

Here's the same information arranged in a different format.

The principal decided to emphasize his educational background and expand on his administrative experience.

Note the use of a chronological sequence to the data presented.

♦ Planned and implemented a $1.5 million school renovation project.

♦ Developed and received a $10,000 grant for student dropout prevention program.

♦ Designed a student dropout prevention program resulting in a 20 percent decrease in high school dropouts.

♦ Implemented computer-assisted math and reading programs.

This resume format would be helpful to a speaker seeking to develop an introduction for Mr. Carey.

♦ Initiated a differentiated supervision approach to teacher evaluation. Trained master teachers and mentor teachers to assist in this process. Increase in staff teaching skills resulted in higher staff morale and a steady rise in student achievement based on quarterly test results.

♦ Led successful bond drive in two communities resulting in major construction and renovation funding.

Middle School Assistant Principal, Lindley Middle School, Milton, VA, 1980-1985.

Don't worry if your resume is longer than one page. Here's where you might deviate from the business model.

♦ Assistant principal of a 1000 student, 60 faculty and staff rural middle school.

♦ Supervised and evaluated certified staff.

♦ Developed hands-on science curriculum for students at risk.

♦ Managed grade reporting, attendance, and permanent records systems.

♦ Responsible for student disciplinary procedures and follow-up with teachers and parents.

If it takes more than one page to present a complete picture of your qualifications then do so.

♦ Worked closely with community agencies involved with alcohol and drug prevention programs.

TEACHING EXPERIENCE:

Physics Teacher, Tremont High School, Patchogue, NY, 1978-1979

- Taught Physics, Science Research, and Advanced Placement (AP) Physics

- Organized School Science Fair

Math Teacher, South Ocean Junior High, Medford, NY, 1975-1978.

- Taught General Math, Pre-Algebra, and Algebra.

- Coached junior varsity basketball.

ACTIVITIES AND AFFILIATIONS:

- Strategic Planning Committee Member, 1996

- President, New York Association of High School Principals, 1990-1992.

There's no rule that says your resume can't be one-page front and back.

Exercise C8-1
IT'S YOUR TURN

Find your resume and take a hard look. Using the Do's and Don'ts suggested in this module to assess your paper image for the following points:

- Error-free, exceptionally legible, and eye-appealing resume

- Clearly visible headings that boldly announce your skills

- Accomplishment statements that sell your results, not job duties

- Effective writing that's clear, concise, and correct

- A professional image

SUMMARY

Don't wait to prepare a resume until the unexpected happens when a colleague asks for your resume so you can be properly introduced or needs it to complete the application process for your nomination to a community advisory board. Your resume is a professional account of your authentic abilities, current skills, and school-related accomplishments. Today's technology can help you revise your resume as your career develops. The objective is to keep a CURRENT, positive, and accurate document that verifies and projects you as a professional educator.

References

Anthony, R. and Roe, G. (1994). *101 grade A resumes for teachers*. New York: Barron's Educational Series.

Eyler, D. (1990). *Resumes that mean business*. New York: Random House.

Jackson, T. (1990). The perfect resume. New York: Doubleday.

Marino, K. (1990). The resume guide for women of the '90s. Santa Barbara, CA: Tangerine Press.

Simon, J. (1981). How to write a resume. In *Business Communication*, Golen S., Figgins, R., and Smeltzer, L. (Eds.) (1984). New York: John Wiley & Sons, pp. 233-236.

Resource

The Perfect Resume Computer Kit
Tom Jackson and Bill Buckingham
Permax Systems/Madison WI 53716/Tel: 608-222-8804

PART THREE

INITIATING THE DEVELOPMENT PROCESS

COMPETENCY NINE

DESIGNING YOUR PROFESSIONAL DEVELOPMENT PLAN

"Today's preparation determines tomorrow's achievement."
—NASSP Great Quotations

COMPETENCY STATEMENT

Stay current with professional advancements and changes, by adopting systematic ways to assess and build the continued development of job knowledge and skills.

KNOWLEDGE BASE HIGHLIGHTS

Schein 1978. Successful managers study the complexities of their career development from both an individual and an organizational perspective. The reflective leader analyzes his or her changing needs throughout the adult life cycle.

McCall, Lombardo, & Morrison 1989. Effective leaders take charge of their development and devise ways to help others within the organization to develop their skills. It requires a commitment to lifelong learning and involves continuing effort.

McCall 1994. "The principal's main job is to develop with colleagues purpose and direction, and to move adults and students toward achieving that shared vision." This process demands that the principal develop a host of competencies, clearly defined and clearly assessed. "Making a principal involves much learning."

The following guidelines are offered to help you in designing your written communication professional development plan. Professional development is a continuous process involving personal planning, action and energy. Outlined in this section is a step-by-step process to help you identify training needs, consider the numerous resources available to you, and establish an action plan for self and school improvement in the skill area of written expression.

Step One:	Consider previous performance evaluations, results from any other writing assessment, and other material that may be helpful in planning for self- and school improvement.
Step Two:	Revisit the textbook exercises and workbook training modules. Identify specific behaviors in which you show strength and those for which you desire growth.
Step Three:	After examining the specific behaviors within each area where growth is targeted, narrow the list to ten or fewer.
Step Four:	Narrow the list to three behaviors that are top priority for immediate action; identify two behaviors that are next in importance to you. Develop objectives for each behavior.
Step Five:	For each priority behavior you have recorded as requiring immediate attention, review the resources in each chapter or module to find books, articles, seminars, and activities to assist you in meeting your objectives.
Step Six:	Using the resources you chose in Step Five, identify actions you will take to improve or strengthen a targeted behavior. Set a specific deadline date and identify who you will involve to help you complete this action.
Step Seven:	Monitor your progress to keep yourself motivated and provide opportunities to recognize your successes. Revise and make changes to your plan as needed.

STEP ONE: WRITING PERFORMANCE ASSESSMENT

The following outline can be used to review and summarize any previous information you have about your written communication effectiveness.

A. List the performance evaluations you have gathered and specify your writing strengths and growth areas.

EVALUATION	STRENGTHS	TRAINING NEEDS	PERSONAL COMMENTS
1			
2			

B. List results from performance assessment instruments used in the textbook and the workbook to target strength and growth areas.

EVALUATION	STRENGTHS	TRAINING NEEDS	PERSONAL COMMENTS
1			
2			

C. Cite results from other sources such as colleagues or professional workshops.

EVALUATION	STRENGTHS	TRAINING NEEDS	PERSONAL COMMENTS
1			
2			

Step Two: Identifying Specific Strengths and Improvement Areas

The effective behaviors summarized here are based on the text, *Written Expression,* which is the companion guide to the workbook.

EFFECTIVE BEHAVIORS IN WRITTEN EXPRESSION

PART ONE: CHALLENGING THE STATUS QUO	Strength Area	Growth Area
1: Fostering Open Communication		
1. Establishing an inviting school office environment.		
2. Training a courteous office staff.		
3. Producing high-quality school documents.		
4. Keeping the school-community informed.		
5. Developing school-community relationships.		
6. Collaborating on school writing projects.		
7. Using the writing process to develop complex documents.		
8. Designing a school-community public relations plan.		
2: Checking Your Communication Competence		
1. Reducing your writing apprehension.		
2. Practicing effective writing behaviors.		
3. Eliminating common writing problems.		
4. Improving the school's communication effectiveness.		

PART TWO DISPLAYING AUDIENCE SAVVY	Strength Area	Growth Area
3. Writing to Staff		
1. Establishing your purpose.		
2. Making your writing sound personal.		
3. Keeping memos and letters brief.		
4. Avoiding repetition.		
5. Adopting the right tone.		
6. Using strong topic sentences.		
7. Eliminating clutter.		
8. Avoiding jargon		
4: Writing to Parents		
1. Creating a favorable impression.		
2. Assessing the needs of the parent.		
3. Writing bad news sensitively.		
4. Using a specific organizational strategy.		
5. Determining your purpose.		
6. Writing the way you speak.		
5: Writing to Central Office Staff		
1. Clarifying your writing purpose.		
2. Using the 5 W's and H to organize details.		
3. Deciding how much information to convey.		
4. Keeping the boss informed.		
5. Keeping memos and letters brief and clear.		
6. Paying attention to detail and appearance.		
7. Knowing how the boss perceives your writing effectiveness.		
6: Writing to Peers		
1. Assessing your peer relationships.		
2. Sharing your writing products.		
3. Asking for feedback on your writing.		
4. Keeping the communication channels open.		
5. Coaching your peers for job success.		

	Strength Area	Growth Area
7: Writing to Your Local Community		
1. Identifying the key communicators in the community.		
2. Establishing regular communication channels.		
3. Surveying the local community.		
4. Creating a school with a unifying purpose.		
5. Involving all stakeholders in the educational process.		
6. Establishing a working relationship with news reporters.		
7. Writing news releases and articles about the school.		
8: Writing to Your Professional Community		
1. Developing articles for professional journals.		
2. Using mindmaps to generate topic ideas.		
3. Using visual graphic organizers to develop content.		
4. Writing articles for local publications.		
PART THREE: COMMUNICATION THAT MEANS BUSINESS		
9: Sharpening Your Writing Skills		
1. Writing clearly and concisely. Using short words, sentences, and paragraphs.		
2. Writing correctly. Using proper grammar, punctuation, and spelling.		
3. Eliminating unnecessary detail. Asking the reader what information is needed.		
4. Writing with style.		
5. Using visuals to illustrate important points.		
6. Editing your writing carefully.		
7. Choosing the right word to send the intended message.		

	Strength Area	Growth Area
10: Attacking Your In-Basket		
1. Knowing various writing purposes and forms.		
2. Writing effective memos and letters.		
3. Developing persuasive reports.		
4. Using computer technology to develop a resource file of school letters, memos, and reports..		
5. Creating effective school newsletters.		
6. Designing brochures, flyers, and posters.		
7. Fostering two-way communication through surveys and questionnaires.		
8. Keeping a current, professional resume.		
9. Allocating job time for writing tasks.		
10. Using your office staff to help organize and prioritize writing tasks.		

STEP THREE: NARROWING YOUR GROWTH TARGET

Review the growth areas checked above. List ten behaviors that you feel need immediate attention.

Chapter	Behavior
1.	
2.	
3.	
4.	
5.	
6.	
7.	

8.	
9.	
10.	

STEP FOUR: SELECTING TOP PRIORITY WRITING BEHAVIORS

Think about what specific behaviors are critical to your current job situation. Then identify the skills that will be important in the near future. Based on this analysis choose five writing behaviors that are top priority for you.

1. _____

2. _____

3. _____

4. _____

5. _____

STEP FIVE: CHOOSING DEVELOPMENT ACTIVITIES

Now that you have identified your priorities, your next step is to select possible activities and experiences. Tailor your activities to your learning style. Are you a reflective learner or a doer? Do you learn best by modeling a behavior or reading about it? Consider the range of opportunities available to you:

- ◆ On the job opportunities
- ◆ Modeling others who have the desired skill
- ◆ Taking workshops and courses
- ◆ Reading books, articles, and technical guides
- ◆ Practicing the skill and getting feedback from trusted colleagues
- ◆ Modeling the way for staff and peers

TARGETED BEHAVIOR	DEVELOPMENTAL ACTIVITY
1.	
2.	
3.	
4.	
5.	

Step Six and Step Seven: Designing an Action Plan and Monitoring Your Progress

Building on strengths is part of your professional development. Review the behaviors you checked as strength areas. Develop your action plan for your top three.

Template C9-1. PDP Writing Guide

STRENGTHS TARGETED	ACTION PLANS	INVOLVEMENT OF OTHERS	COMPLETION DATES
STRENGTH OBJECTIVES:			
STRENGTH OBJECTIVES:			
STRENGTH OBJECTIVES:			

Please record the development needs you have chosen for improvement. Write specific objectives and action plans for each objective. Remember to involve others and set dates for completion.

DEVELOPMENT NEEDS TARGETED	ACTION PLANS	INVOLVE- MENT OF OTHERS	COMPLETION DATES
NEED OBJECTIVES:			
NEED OBJECTIVES:			
NEED OBJECTIVES:			

TEMPLATE C9-2. SAMPLE PDP

DEVELOPMENT NEEDS TARGETED	ACTION PLANS	INVOLVE-MENT OF OTHERS	COMPLETION DATES
NEED Preparing clear and concise letters and memos. **OBJECTIVES:**			
Eliminate lengthy memos and letters.	1. Write a purpose statement before starting a draft.	None	Ongoing
Involve secretary and assistant principal.	2. Assess the needs of my reader. Determine the right tone.	None	
Use my computer more often.	3. Adopt a specific organizational strategy to get my message across.	None	
	4. Use my computer to check for spelling, grammatical, and readability problems.	None	Ongoing Evaluate quarterly
	5. Keep draft to one page. Keep sentences and paragraphs short.	None	Ongoing Evaluate weekly
	6. Ask a colleague to read for clarity and tone.	Staff	
	7. Start a template file	Secretary	Evaluate annually

References

McCall, J. (1994). *The principal's edge.* Princeton Junction, NJ: Eye On Education.

McCall, M., Lombardi, M. and Morrison, A. (1989). *The lessons of experience: How successful executives develop on the job.* Lexington, MA: Lexington Books.

Schein, E. (1978). *Career dynamics: Matching individual and organizational needs.* Reading, MA: Addison-Wesley.

EPILOGUE

INSIDE THE PRINCIPAL'S OFFICE

Mr. Bentley, the principal of Anywhere School, has had a terrible day. His morning began with a stalled engine just after he left home and he was already running late. Frustration mounted when he got to the school parking lot and found his parking place taken by an unknown car.

That was just the beginning. Things continued downhill: two very irate bus drivers waited to see him as he entered the main office, a dozen urgent phone calls from the PTA president, the staff newsletters late from the printer, and two teachers absent with only one substitute available.

And on top of this, the superintendent called and wanted ASAP a revised copy of his annual report and a current resume so he could nominate Bill for a leadership position to the local elementary principals association.

Bill Bentley took a deep breath and began jotting down the things that needed his immediate attention and those things he could delegate. He called in his assistant principal and asked her to cover a class until a substitute could be obtained. Before he dealt with the bus drivers and the urgent phone calls, he asked his secretary to do the following:

♦ Use her clerical assistant to find a substitute.

♦ Print out a copy of the latest annual report.

♦ Sort through the incoming mail and prioritize.

♦ Draft any memos or letters that were routine in nature by pulling up similar requests from the school correspondence template file.

After resolving the early morning events, Bill called the superintendent to confirm the exact information he wanted revised in the annual report and the due date of the report and resume. At 9:30, after checking his e-mail, Bill informed his secretary that he would be observing in the classrooms until 10:30. He got an update on the status of getting a substitute and the work correspondence he requested earlier. His secretary told him she would have his in-basket ready by 10:30 when he returned to the office.

At 10:45 he reentered his office and found his mail and incoming paperwork arranged in several neat packets marked as signature only, routine memos and letters/not urgent, special memos and letters marked urgent, and a to-do list of upcoming deadlines for reports and projects. He reviewed the packet of memos and letters labeled urgent. He handled several of the items by phone and redirected one to his assistant principal for more information. With the remaining three items he began drafting his thoughts for each response on Action Planning Sheets.

With the preliminary work done on the high-priority items, Bill quickly scanned the packet of school forms requiring his signature and the routine memos and letters drafted by his secretary. He modified them as needed and returned them to her for final changes and printing as he exited the office to monitor the school lunch and visit with teachers and students.

At 1:00 p.m. he checked with his assistant principal and directed her to handle any emerging problems while he completed his paperwork from 1:00 until 2:30 p.m. Bill then returned to his office to draft the important memos and letters he worked on earlier. Using his template file, Bill pulled up on his screen similar letters and began to complete these items that needed a written response. By 2:30 he had composed each document; he then asked his secretary to review them for clarity and to make any suggestions.

The buses started to roll in and Mr. Bentley went outside to chat with several of the drivers. He ended his afternoon with an unexpected parent conference and several short unannounced visits from teachers as they wrapped up their day. By 3:30 he returned to his office to finish up any remaining paperwork. He quickly opened his template resume file and added a recent presentation he made at a national conference and printed the document. Then he reread his annual report and began to generate the information he needed to complete the revisions to the report within the next two days.

At 4:00 p.m. Bill scooped up his tennis racket, gave his secretary the list of items needed to complete his report revisions for her to compile, and headed for the courts at the nearby high school. Bill was not taking his in-basket home after an exhausting day at the office. Having planned how to attack his writing tasks and using the resources available to him, Bill is no longer at home, ALONE.

What's on the Disk?

Packaged on the back cover of this Workbook are two diskettes: one in Macintosh format, the other for Windows/Windows '95. Each of the folders ("directories" for Windows 3.1 users) corresponds to one of the *Competency Training Modules* in Part Two of this workbook. Each file contains one of the documents or templates displayed in the workbook or in the accompanying hardcover book, *Written Expression: The Principal's Survival Guide* (ISBN 1-883001-34-X).

Folder C1
(COMPETENCY ONE: MEMOS)

Workbook

File	Page	Purpose	Audience	Tone	Strategy
C1-1.doc	37	To persuade	Staff	Supportive	Need/Plan/Benefit
C1-2.doc	40	To announce	Staff	Collaborative	Five W's
C1-3.doc	42	To inform	Peers	Objective	Topic/Chronological
C1-4.doc	44	To reprimand	Teacher	Authoritative	Problem/Solutions
C1-5.doc	47	Memo template guide			

Hardcover

File	Page	Purpose	Audience	Tone	Strategy
F5-2.doc	84	To explain/justify	Superintendent	Objective	Topic
F6-1.doc	96	To request	Peer	Collaborative	Problem/Solution
F6-2.doc	97	To persuade	Peer	Objective	Need/Plan/Benefit
F6-3.doc	97	To instruct	Peer	Supportive	Chronological
F6-4.doc	98	To congratulate	Peer	Complimentary	Topic
F6-5.doc	98	To respond to concern	Superintendent	Objective	Chronological
F6-6.doc	99	To show sympathy	Peer	Supportive	Topic
F10-5.doc	144	To inform	Superintendent	Objective	Topic

Folder C2
(COMPETENCY TWO: BUSINESS LETTERS)

Workbook

File	Page	Purpose	Audience	Tone	Strategy
C2-1.doc	56	To recommend	Peer	Complimentary	Inductive/Topic
C2-2.doc	59	To request action	Community	Authoritative	Problem/Solution
C2-3.doc	61	To give bad news	Parent	Businesslike	Deductive/Topic
C2-4.doc	63	To congratulate	Peer	Friendly	Topic
C2-5.doc	65	To evaluate	Colleague	Objective	Analytical/Topic
C2-6.doc	69	Letter template guide			

Hardcover

File	Page	Purpose	Audience	Tone	Strategy
F4-3.doc	66	To give bad news	Parent	Objective	Inductive
F4-5.doc	68	To inform	Parent/ Neutral	Objective	Problem/Solution
F4-6.doc	69	To inform	Parent/ Positive	Friendly	Inductive
F4-7.doc	70	To inform	Parent/ Negative	Assertive	Problem/Solution Chronological
F10-7.doc	149	To allay concern	Parent	Objective	Question and Answer

Folder C3
(COMPETENCY THREE: REPORTS)

Workbook

File	Page	Purpose	Audience	Tone	Strategy
C3-1.doc	86	To persuade	Funding Agency	Businesslike	Topic/RFP

Hardcover

File	Page	Purpose	Audience	Tone	Strategy
F10-9.doc	155	To describe/ clarify thinking	Teacher	Objective	Inductive/Topic

Folder C4
(COMPETENCY FOUR: SCHOOL FORMS, NOTES, AWARDS, AND BUMPER STICKERS)

Workbook

File	Page	Purpose	Audience	Tone	Strategy
C4-1.doc	97	To build relationships/ inform	Parents	Friendly	Topic
C4-2.doc	98	To motivate	Staff	Collaborative	Topic
C4-3.doc	99	To inform	Parents	Collaborative	Need/Plan/Benefit
C4-4.doc	101	To suspend	Parent	Objective	Topic/Deductive
C4-5.doc	102	To evaluate	Staff	Objective	Topic/Inductive
C4-6.doc	104	To evaluate	Staff	Objective	Topic/Inductive
C4-7.doc	107	To inform	Parents	Objective	Topic
C4-8.doc	109	To recommend	Peer	Supportive	Topic
C4-9.doc	110	To give recognition	Staff	Appreciative	
C4-10.doc	111	To give recognition	Staff	Appreciative	
C4-11.doc	111	To publicize	Parent/ Community	Supportive	

Folder C5
(COMPETENCY FIVE: NEWS ARTICLES, PRESS RELEASES, AND TOP NOTCH-NEWSLETTERS)

Workbook

File	Page	Purpose	Audience	Tone	Strategy
C5-1.doc	116	To inform	Community	Objective	5 W's
C5-2.doc	117	To inform	Community	Objective	5 W's
C5-3.doc	119	To seek data	Staff	Objective	Topic
C5-4.doc	120	To announce	Community	Objective	5 W's

Folder C6
(COMPETENCY SIX: BROCHURES, BULLETINS, FLYERS AND POSTERS)

Workbook

File	Page	Purpose	Audience	Tone	Strategy
C6-1.doc	134	To persuade	Parents	Collaborative	Topic
C6-2.doc	135	To persuade	Parents	Humorous	5 W's
C6-3.doc	136	To inform	Parents/Community	Objective	Topic
C6-4.doc	139	Brochure Template			

Folder C7
(COMPETENCY SEVEN: SURVEYS AND QUESTIONNAIRES)

Workbook

File	Page	Purpose	Audience	Tone	Strategy
C7-1.doc	146	To improve instruction; build relationships	Students	Collaborative	Forced Choice Topic
C7-2.doc	147	To foster school improvement; build relationships	Parents	Collaborative	Open Ended/ Topic
C7-3.doc	149	To foster school improvement; encourage team building	Staff	Collaborative	Combination Format/Topic
C7-4.doc	153	To seek feedback on leadership style	Staff	Objective/ Humorous	Forced Choice/ Topic

Folder C8
(COMPETENCY EIGHT: GRADE A RESUMES)

Workbook

File	Page	Purpose	Audience	Tone	Strategy
C8-1.doc	159	To inform/persuade	Personnel Director	Objective	Competency/ Topic Format
C8-2.doc	161	To inform/persuade	Colleague	Objective	Chronological Format

HOW TO USE THE DISK

Packaged on the back cover of this workbook are two diskettes: one in Macintosh format, the other for Windows/Windows '95. The files may be opened using most word processing packages.

Each of the folders ("directories" for Windows 3.1 users) corresponds to one of the *Competency Training Modules* in Part Two of this workbook. Each file contains one of the documents or templates displayed in this workbook or in the accompanying hard-cover book, *Written Expression: The Principals' Survival Guide* (ISBN 1-883001-34-X).

On page 181 of the workbook, you will find "What's on the Disk?" which lists all the folders and files on the disk, cross-referenced to the appropriate pages in the books. After you open one of these files, the document will appear on your computer's screen, allowing you to work interactively with the material in this workbook and build a document file of your own.

You are welcome to copy the files, customize them, save them under other names, and otherwise use them to enhance the quality of your professional writing.

Writing can be easy. Explore your potential!

For Product Safety Concerns and Information please contact our EU
representative GPSR@taylorandfrancis.com Taylor & Francis Verlag GmbH,
Kaufingerstraße 24, 80331 München, Germany

Printed and bound by CPI Group (UK) Ltd, Croydon, CR0 4YY
08/06/2025
01896981-0010